East Lincolnshire's Lost Railways

Louth's Jacobean-style station seen at its best on 14 August 1965 - surely one of the most elegant buildings on the Great Northern Railway system.
J. Wrottesley/A. Ludlam Collection.

An early scene at Boston prior to the extension of the water tower with Stirling 8ft Single No. 221 leaving the station.

The Lincolnshire Wolds Railway Society would like to thank Alan Stennett and Phil Eldridge for giving their time to compile this publication. Thank you also to Howard Johnston, Leyland Penn, Mike Franklin, Michael Stewart, Mary Cook, David Enefer and Colin Epton for their contributions, and to the family of the late Alf Ludlam for donating the photographic collection that was key to the project.

Printed by Allinson Print & Supplies, Allinson House, Lincoln Way, Fairfield Industrial Estate, Louth, Lincolnshire LN11 0LS

Issue 1. September 2020.

East Lincolnshire's Lost Railways

Alan Stennett

LWRS PUBLICATIONS

Published by the
Lincolnshire Wolds Railway Society

Britannia Pacific No. 70041 'Sir John Moore' about to cross the Grand Sluice Bridge at Boston with a King's Cross-Cleethorpes express on 5 June 1962. *G. Brown Collection.*

Contents

In a scene from the late 1940s, well-known local Postman, E. A. Brown, is pictured with a loaded barrow on Firsby station's up platform. One of Mr Brown's regular duties was the safe loading of mail onto the trains and the transfer of mail between trains.
G. Brown Collection.

Introduction

In the early part of the 20th century Lincolnshire had a comprehensive railway system. There were very few communities more than a few miles from the nearest railway station, all offering connections within the county and beyond. By the middle years of that century, the damage to the system during the First World War and competition from cars, buses and lorries was rendering many of those stations and lines uneconomic, with some services withdrawn as early as the 1930s.

The urgent need for reliable transport during the Second World War kept most of the lines in service, and nationalisation and a boom in travel after the war saw most of the county's railways continue to serve their communities. However, within ten years of the end of the conflict, the decline resumed and accelerated, with more passenger services in particular withdrawn from the county.

In an effort to restore profitability, the Government appointed Dr Richard Beeching to advise on a reorganisation of the railway system. His report, in 1963, recommended the closure of many routes in Lincolnshire, and the part of the county to the south and east of Lincoln was particularly hard hit. Most of the lines in the area were closed, along with many stations on the ones that remained open.

The routes most affected were the Lincolnshire Loop Line, from Peterborough to Lincoln by way of Spalding and Boston, and the East Lincolnshire Railway, which left the Loop at Boston to continue to Grimsby by way of Louth and Alford. The two companies were incorporated into the London and North Eastern Railway in the Grouping of 1923, and of the Eastern Region of British Railways on nationalisation in 1947. Large parts of both closed on the same day, 5 October 1970, along with a number of branch lines served by them. Those are the lines that will be covered in this book.

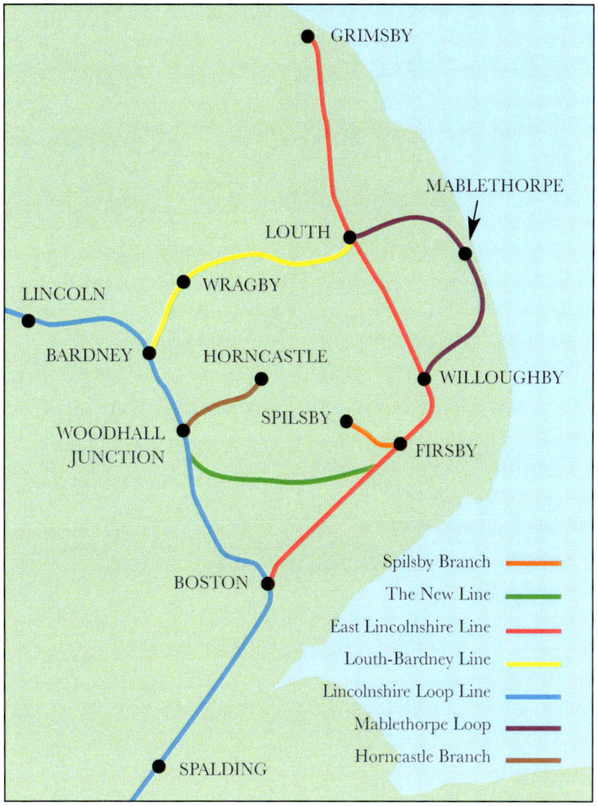

A Cravens 2-Car Diesel Multiple Unit on a service for Sheffield calls at Stixwould in August 1970. *P. Grey/A. Ludlam Collection.*

The Lincolnshire Loop Line of the Great Northern Railway

The Lincolnshire Loop was one of the results of a series of proposals, Parliamentary plans and company mergers and takeovers. Several companies put forward plans for lines between London and York, some with routes that included ones passing through Cambridge, continuing through Lincolnshire to the north, while others preferred the option of a direct line to Peterborough, with alternative routes going through Lincoln or directly north along the Trent Valley. Eventually, three of the competing companies, the Cambridge and York, the Direct Northern and the Wakefield, Lincoln and Boston came together under the name of the Great Northern Railway. They agreed on a single route from London to Peterborough, with two lines continuing north. The one element, known as the Towns Line, serving Grantham, Newark and Doncaster, opened in 1852 and became what we now know as the East Coast Main Line. It is still a key part of the UK's railway infrastructure, but is outside the scope of this book. Our interest is in the second line, the Lincolnshire Loop Line, which ran north through the county, serving Spalding, Boston, Lincoln and Gainsborough before continuing on to Retford initially and Doncaster later.

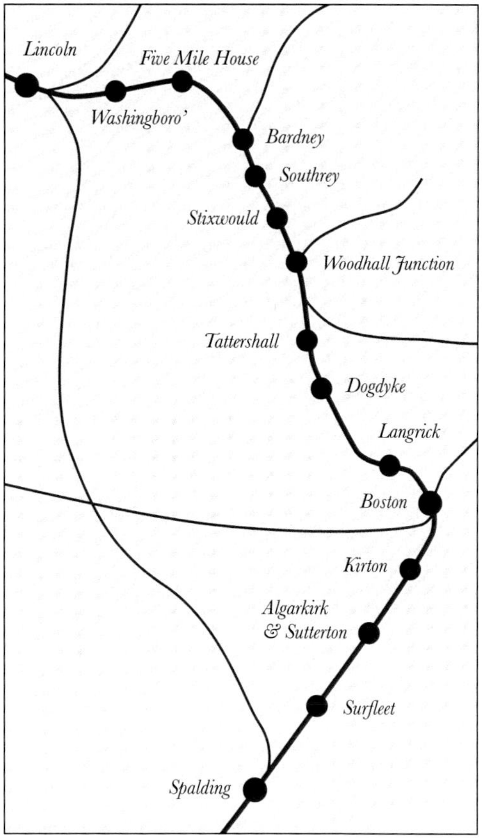

It was an important line to the county, because it linked so many of the bigger towns as well as a large number of smaller communities. It remains in service between Peterborough and Spalding, although the intermediate stations at Peakirk, Deeping St Nicholas and Littleworth have all been closed.

The station at Spalding is still open after a determined local campaign reversed Dr Beeching's decision to end passenger traffic there, and is a key railhead for south-east Lincolnshire, with a connection to Lincoln and points further north along the later Great Northern and Great Eastern Joint line. From Spalding the Lincolnshire Loop continued across the Fens to Boston, through stations at Surfleet, Algarkirk and Sutterton and Kirton. This section was closed and lifted, although the modern traveller can still enjoy the fenland scenery, since much of the old trackbed was used for a new alignment of the A16 trunk road.

Boston station continues to serve the town, although trains follow the route of the Boston, Sleaford and Midland Counties Railway from Sleaford and Grantham. They continue along a small stretch of the old East Lincolnshire Railway connecting to what had been the Wainfleet and Firsby Railway branch to Skegness. The Loop line crossed the River Witham at Boston on the Grand Sluice Bridge before turning onto the east bank of the river, following a route surveyed for the Wakefield, Lincoln and Boston. The GNR had purchased the Witham Navigation, and built much of the line on the banks of the river, saving money by using Navigation-owned land. It followed the river to Lincoln, passing through Langrick, Dogdyke, Tattershall, Kirkstead (later renamed Woodhall Junction), Stixwould, Southrey, Bardney, Five Mile House and Washingborough on its way to the city. Two branches were served by stations on this section. The Horncastle branch, through Woodhall Spa to Horncastle, left at Kirkstead, which was also the junction for the 1913 'New Line' to Firsby, and the Louth to Bardney branch which ran across the Wolds between those two communities. Both branches closed to passengers in the 1950s, followed by complete closure of the through route and the New Line in 1970, although the section between Boston and Woodhall Junction lost its services in 1963, seven years before the main closures.

An early photo at Dogdyke showing the ferry and station alongside the River Witham. *H. Rundell/A. Ludlam Collection.*

North of Lincoln, the line continued to Doncaster, and is still in use as part of what became the GN&GE Joint line.

Construction and operation

The Great Northern received Royal Assent for its plans on 26 June 1846 and took an immediate decision to concentrate on the Lincolnshire loop. They knew it would be easier to build across flat stretches of Lincolnshire rather than through the hills south of Grantham, and getting some tracks in place would ensure at least some income for the company. In these days of interminable delays before any construction project gets under way, it is startling to realise that the company expected trains to be running in just over a year, although it actually took one year more than that, with the section between Peterborough and Lincoln opening on 17 October 1848, four years before the Towns Line.

Work preparing the route started in Lincoln and along the River Witham in late 1846 and between Peterborough and Spalding in September of the following year. Materials were shipped in through the

Spalding became a major junction on the Lincs Loop, with lines from March, Lincoln, Bourne and Sutton Bridge converging there in GNR days. *S. Gibbard.*

ports of Boston and Gainsborough, with much use being made of the GN-owned Witham Navigation between Boston and Lincoln. Ironically, the boost in water-borne trade was short-lived, since the railway, once opened took away much of the existing business – quite deliberately in the case of the Witham Navigation. Special cheap fares in converted 'standing-only' cattle wagons were aimed at killing off the passenger trade in the small steam packet boats on the river. It would seem that cost was not the sole objective of the travellers – the boats stayed in service for more than a decade after the cheap trains were introduced.

Construction was almost entirely done by men with picks and shovels, many of whom would have been farmworkers from the area attracted by the better wages offered by the contractors. There were occasional problems – a strike of workmen at Lincoln was caused by the failures of one of the sub-contractors to pay his men, and there were reports of manpower shortages in the summer months when the chance of better rates in the harvest fields tempted some away.

As in many other parts of the country, the arrival of the railways in Lincolnshire was a boon to many locals unhappy with working on the land. In addition to the ones who helped build the lines, new career opportunities opened for others. Working as a clerk, a porter or on a permanent way gang was more secure and usually better paid, although not dramatically so. Retired railwayman George Holden joined the GNR in 1920 at Dogdyke as a probationary junior clerk on one pound and three pence a week (£1.01), as a better bet than the 13/- (65p) he was earning on the land. He still described them as 'hard times'.

"I didn't get onto the staff for another three years, and that was only after going to London for a written examination, a full medical and an interview with the directors. I had to stand in front of the table for the whole of that meeting, and they looked at you as if you were a lower form of life!"

Once on the staff, promotion prospects were good, and Les Camm, who joined in the 1920s, said railway workers – nearly always men before WW1 – had a certain status, particularly in villages with stations.

"The station master was a person of some note – equivalent to the vicar or the local doctor, and other railwaymen were seen as having a certain status in the community, often involved in other local organisations – definitely a step up from farm workers."

The lines from Peterborough to Boston ran almost dead straight across the Fens, with the only major engineering works being the construction of many bridges and culverts over the waterways in the area. The three largest bridges, that over Vernatt's Drain at Spalding and two over the Witham at Boston and Horsley Deeps, near Bardney, were all built of timber. A fire on the Vernatt's bridge caused the company to station a watchman to guard against a similar problem on the half-mile long Bardney structure, the largest built by the GN. Such concerns were also likely to have led to the later decision to rebuild all three with iron components.

There were major initial difficulties with the bridge at Boston. The Great Northern and the East Lincolnshire originally intended to cross the river by separate structures, but a decision that both would share the same one didn't solve the problem. The Admiralty, who were responsible for the tidal part of the river in Boston, refused to allow a bridge to cross it, and landowners near the final site battled with the companies about land ownership and compensation, disputes that were finally settled in court.

Boston might also have played an even bigger part in the development of railways in the area. As well as the usual facilities for goods and passengers, it was a major engineering and construction centre, with a large civil engineers yard, a gas works and timber creosoting equipment. Most important, it had a locomotive department, which, it was hoped, would become the main works for the company. Sadly for Boston, pressure from Edmund Dennison, vice-chairman of the GNR, saw the locomotive department moved to his home-town of Doncaster in 1853, losing Boston a valuable industry and many well-paid jobs.

In contrast to the straight run across the Fens, the stretch along the Witham was more sinuous. The purchase of the Navigation by the company meant it could lay tracks on its own land for much of the route, but only if they literally built on the banks. The river had

Class B17 4-6-0 No. 61638 'Melton Hall' approaches Boston with a Doncaster to March local in June 1958. *A. Ludlam Collection.*

been straightened by drainage and navigation improvements in the 18th century, but it was still far from a straight line. Trains were limited to 40mph in later years, with 20mph restrictions at a number of places. The tracks were also liable to be flooded on occasion. One goods train driver reported that while his steam locomotive had no problems, and he and his fireman kept their feet dry, their guard was in danger of being washed out of his brake van by the bow wave of water flowing through the doors at the front and back. He kept dry by standing on his seat until the train reached 'dry land'.

Another complication along this stretch was the number of ferries that crossed the river. Each had been the responsibility of the Navigation, and that duty passed onto the railway company. Each station was situated close to a bridge or ferry which had served the adjacent community. There had been a bridge at Tattershall for many centuries, and the GN paid all or part of the costs of new structures at Kirkstead, Bardney and Langrick, but Washingborough, Five Mile House, Southrey, Stixwould and Dogdyke continued to be served by the ferries up to the closure of the line, and sometimes for a period afterwards. Norman Clark commented that although he had joined the railway in 1925 as a lad porter at Five Mile House, most of his work was as a ferryman.

Table 52 PETERBOROUGH (North), SPALDING, BOSTON, and LINCOLN (via Boston)

Miles		Week Days														Sun.		
		aft	mrn	mrn	mrn	mrn	mrn	mrn	aft	mrn	aft	aft	aft V	aft	aft	mrn	aft	aft
	1 London (King'sC.) dep	11F15		4 15	..	..	..	7 23	..	1010	1 10	..	4 5	..	5§50	1010	..	6 5
—	Peterboro' (North). dep	3 0	..	6 35	..	..	..	1054	..	1 45	3 0	Skegness to Lincoln	5 57	To Horncastle arr. 7 46 aft. (Table 53)	7 50	1 35	..	8 0
5¼	Peakirk	mrn	..	..	..	..	..	11 5	..	1 56	..		..		8 [illegible]	aft	..	..
7	St. James Deeping B	..	..	..	..	..	..	11 9	..	2 0	..		..		8 5	..	..	..
11½	Littleworth	..	..	..	..	..	..	1117	..	2 8	..		..		8 13	..	..	..
16½	Spalding arr	3 23	..	6 58	..	..	..	1126	..	2 17	3 23		6 21		8 22	2 0	..	8 24
	Spalding dep	3 33	..	7 10	..	Skegness to Lincoln	..	1134	..	2 21	3 28		6 25		8 34	2 5	..	8 32
20½	Surfleet	..	..	7 18	..		..	1142	..	2 29	..		..		8 42	2 13	..	..
24¼	Algarkirk & Sutterton	..	..	7 25	..		..	1149	..	2 36	..		..		8 49	2 20	..	..
27	Kirton	..	..	7 31	..		..	1155	..	2 42	..		..		8 55	2 26	..	..
31	Boston arr	3 52	..	7 39	..		..	12 3	..	2 50	3 48		6 46		9 3	2 34	..	8 53
	Boston dep	..	6 25	..	7 51		1110	Stop	1 40	..	4 10		..	6 57	..	..	2 46	..
35¾	Langrick	..	..	..	8 0		1119		1 49	..	4 19		..	7 6	..	..	2 55	..
42	Dogdyke	..	Aa	..	8 10		1129	..	1 59	..	4 29		..	7 16	..	..	3 5	..
42¾	Tattershall	..	Aa	..	8 13		1132	aft	2 2	..	4 32		..	7 19	..	..	3 11	..
46½	Woodhall Junction..arr	..	6 54	..	8 20		1139	T	2 9	..	4 39		..	7 26	..	..	3 18	..
—	5) Skegness dep	..	..	..	..	7 50	..	1220	..	..	..	4 0	..	..	..	..	..	..
—	59 Firsby "	..	..	..	..	8 30	..	1255	..	..	..	441	..	..	..	..	..	..
—	Woodhall Junction. dep	..	..	..	8 27	9 20	1141	1 36	2 11	..	4 41	524	..	..	..	..	3 23	..
48½	Stixwould	..	..	..	..	9 25	..	..	2 16	..	4 46	..	..	..	..	..	3 28	..
50¼	Southrey	..	..	..	8 31	9 30	..	..	2 21	..	4 51	..	..	..	..	..	3 33	..
52¾	Bardney arr	..	..	..	8 39	9 35	1151	1 47	2 26	..	4 56	535	..	..	..	..	3 38	..
	Bardney dep	..	..	..	8 41	9 37	1153	1 48	2 28	..	4 58	537	..	..	..	..	3 41	..
56¾	Five Mile House	..	..	..	..	9 45	..	..	2 36	..	..	..	..	..	..	..	3 49	..
59½	Washingborough ¶	..	..	..	..	..	..	..	..	..	..	..	..	..	..	..	..	..
62	Lincoln arr	..	..	..	8 56	9 54	12 8	2 3	2 45	..	5 13	554	..	..	..	..	3 59	..

Aa Calls at Dogdyke 643 and Tattershall 6 46 mrn when required to set down
B Station for Market Deeping (3½ miles)
F Except Saturdays but applies on Sundays
§ Restaurant Car King's Cross to Peterborough
T Thro Carriage, Skegness to Lincoln
Through Carriages
V King's Cross to Cleethorpes arr 8 46 aft (Table 55)
¶ Station closed

For OTHER TRAINS between Spalding and Lincoln, see Table 61

Peterborough North to Lincoln via Boston Timetable from October 1942.

"My first job must have been my most responsible, for I was the sole person in charge of a cross-channel boat!"

The ferry at Washingborough was the location for an unfortunate accident during WW1. A Zeppelin airship had dropped some bombs into fields nearby, and a large number of people tried to use the ferry to view the damage. Sadly, the number was too large, and the boat overturned, resulting in the drowning of two people, a young man and a child. A similar event occurred during WW2, when another of the river ferries overturned while carrying servicemen, several of whom were drowned.

Now-preserved B1 4-6-0 No. 61264 pilots a fellow member of the class through Algarkirk and Sutterton on 6 September 1957. *H. B. Priestley/A. Ludlam Collection.*

The stations on the line were mostly built to a fairly standard design – the company plans specified 'plain and inexpensive', and that was the case for stations such as Stixwould and Surfleet, but Spalding, and most of the medium sized buildings, featured Italianate elements. Three-storey towers with overhanging roofs, blind 'windows' and elaborate brickwork could all be found on many of them. It has been suggested that this was to match the Italianate architecture of King's Cross, but that hardly explains Lincoln's mock-Tudor style or the rather severe classical structure at Boston.

The importance of the line to the local communities was shown by the high level of celebration in Boston at the official opening on 17 October 1848. 2,500 children got tea and buns; tea, and a lecture on 'the benefits of steam propulsion' were enjoyed by 'several hundred' members of the working classes. Their social betters – or at least those who could afford eight shilling and sixpence – enjoyed a ride on a train and 'a grand dinner'. During the dinner, GNR Director Edmund Dennison said the new line would provide an 'imperishable and lasting benefit' to the town. It was an ironic claim, in view of Mr Dennison's later moves to shift the engineering facilities to Doncaster, but perhaps the 21 toasts that were drunk made him a little over-enthusiastic.

Services, perhaps not surprisingly, were somewhat chaotic on that first day of service. The last train of the day, running two hours late, crashed through the level crossing gates at Boston. The gatekeeper had not been told about the delay, and went home at 11pm, thirty minutes after the expected arrival. A few days later, the same thing happened again, this time caused by an unexpectedly early arrival. The gates at Lincoln also suffered damage on several occasions, mainly during shunting operations.

The Illustrated London News described the opening as being carried out 'with great éclat'.

'Two well-filled trains left Peterborough at 6 a.m. and 9 a.m. and were hailed all along the lines by crowds who flocked to see them pass. The train was greeted between Boston and Lincoln with bands of music and masses of people.'

In its early years the line was an important route, particularly after the Lincoln to Gainsborough section of the loop was completed in 1849 and the GN opened

Coningsby Junction signal box. *Author's Collection.*

their own line from London King's Cross to Peterborough in 1850. Before 1850 passengers for London had to change at Peterborough to a different company to continue on to the capital. From that time until the Towns line caught up, it was the GN's main line to the north. 10 passenger trains a day each way used the line, although an average speed of just over 15mph from London to York meant the fastest trip still took nearly seven hours. Among its clients was Queen Victoria, who had the train pause in Lincoln to meet the civic dignitaries, all of whom had to climb into her carriage to meet the Monarch. She had apparently taken a vow not to set foot in Lincoln while the current MP was in place. That gentleman had voted against an allowance for Prince Albert, and Victoria took umbrage at the perceived insult.

After 1852, the line lost much of the through passenger trade and settled down to being an important link within the county rather than further afield, although it continued to be Lincoln's main route to the capital and the north for some years. The section from Peterborough to Boston also saw fast through trains coming off the East Lincolnshire Railway, which joined at Boston. These served towns in the east of the county and the ferries across the Humber, although, as we will see later when discussing the East Lincolnshire Railway, that railway's plans for the ferries didn't quite work out as expected.

Goods remained important throughout the line's existence. A key aim of the builders had been to carry Yorkshire coal to London and heavy coal and other loaded goods trains continued to use the route. This had the

Southrey station waiting shelter, signal box, the station house set at right-angles to the track and the distinctive concrete station nameboard, a scene little changed over the course of its 122 years of active life. Seen here in August 1970, two months before the line closed. *P. Grey/A. Ludlam Collection.*

additional benefit of keeping such slow-moving traffic out of the way of the expresses on the Towns Line. Goods were also vital to all the towns and villages along the route, with coal, agricultural fertiliser and feed stuffs, livestock and general goods handles at every station.

Potatoes were a key commodity at most of the stations on the line, particularly on the southern section. Boston and Spalding were major shippers, but Littleworth had a connection with the private, narrow-gauge potato railway operated by a local farming estate, and Kirton was a marshalling point for the potato traffic. Large amounts of other vegetables were also shipped out from most of these stations, as were bulbs and flowers at the appropriate seasons.

Specialist traffic along the Boston to Lincoln section included sleepers and other treated wood products from the GN's Hall Hills depot just north of Boston. Timber, usually brought into Boston docks from Scandinavia, was taken to the depot, where it was impregnated with creosote by soaking them in the solution under pressure in cylindrical metal tanks. The treated timber was more resistant to weather and rotting, although it became more prone to fire, and the works were badly damaged by a blaze in the 1950s. Production continued until the middle 60s, with treated products shipped out all over the GN and its various successor organisations.

Two large users of goods services were located at Bardney, where a food canning business and a sugar beet factory were built. The canning business was alongside the line to Lincoln, with a siding serving the works. It was opened in 1931 by Messrs. A. W. Foster and Company Ltd, initially to can peas, but was taken over the following year by John Morrell & Co. Ltd, and is usually known as Morrell's factory, although it initially traded as Fosters. They gradually expanded their range of canned products to include gooseberries, strawberries, raspberries, plums, fresh peas, beetroot, celery, beans, carrots and new potatoes. Much of the produce arrived by train, as did the cans for filling and the coal for the factory.

K3 2-6-0 No. 61948 at Langrick with a Doncaster to March train on 19 March 1953. *A. Ludlam Collection.*

The sugar factory opened in 1925, processing sugar beet grown in the area, much of which arrived by train, although some came in by barge on the adjacent River Witham and an increasing amount over the years by lorry or tractor-drawn trailer. Large amounts of coal were needed, which was carried by rail, as were many of the workers. Alf Mettam, working on Bardney station in the 1930s, remembered that the staff travelling to and from Lincoln needed six trains at each change of shift. The products of the factory, which included animal feed as well as the processed sugar, also left by train.

As with most of Lincolnshire's railways, excursion traffic was important on the Loop, with trips to the seaside from Lincoln, Sheffield and other North and East Midlands cities initially travelling down to Boston before reversing back up the East Lincolnshire to Firsby for Skegness and Willoughby or Louth for Sutton on Sea and Mablethorpe. This round-about route was shortened in 1913 by the opening of the New Line from Kirkstead to Firsby.

An important leisure traffic to stations actually on the loop was that of keen fishermen coming to pursue their hobby on the banks of the Witham or of the many fishable drains in the area. Woodhall Junction, Dogdyke, Tattershall and Southrey were particularly noted as the locations for large competitive matches, but all the stations saw many individuals out for a day on the banks.

When matches were taking place, it was not uncommon for special trains to be run – on one noted occasion six specials were housed in the yard at Woodhall Junction, which would have meant that several thousand passengers had travelled down for the event. Families often came too, and locals tell stories of the extra pocket money to be earned by taking a billy-can with dry tea back to their homes, adding boiling water and getting a half-penny for their troubles.

Dogdyke station pictured on 18 May 1959.
H. Priestley/A. Ludlam Collection.

The railway companies themselves ran matches for their own staff. At one match in 1938, 'open to bona fide members of angling associations and angling clubs of the LNER', special trains were run from Yorkshire with free travel for competitors. They were well supported.

'The fifth annual contest for the All Lines Championship took place at Woodhall Jct, in the River Witham, on July 24. Over 400 anglers from Manchester, Mexborough, Sheffield, Doncaster, Retford, Lincoln, Woodhall, Stratford and Boston competed. Weights were below the average for this river, owing to the hot weather and the water being about 4 ft. below normal. Plenty of sport was experienced, but the fish in general were on the small side.'

Sheffield was congratulated on winning the team prize, with one of their members the overall winner.

Betting on such matches was strictly illegal, but it is known that bookmakers travelled down on the train taking bets, retired to the Kings Head at Martin Dales while the event took place, and then paying out again on the return journey.

Fishing specials continued until the lines closed in the 1960s, and competitions still take place today. However, the number of participants is small, and the contestants travel by car and park alongside their 'pegs' or markers.

The Italianate style of several of the larger stations on the Lincolnshire loop is well shown on this photo of Tattershall, including the chamfered roof and massive chimney block. Beet, potatoes, corn and wool were loaded here. Sacks would be hired from the railway company, the weight of the sack being determined by its contents: 19 stones for beans or peas, 18 stones for wheat, 16 stones of barley and 12 stones of oats. These would be manhandled - Fleeces were made into "bales" or "sheets" stitched together with heavy wooden pegs, each "sheet" holding 40 fleeces and were hauled onto farm wagons using wooden planks for their journey to the station. *D. Skinns.*

The career opportunities on the railways continued to prove attractive to young men in the countryside, with moves to other locations key to promotion. The LNER magazine in 1946 marked the progress of Mr F. Bebee on his retirement in 1946.

'Mr Bebee joined the old GNR at Woodhall Junction in 1900 as a lad porter, was moved on to Skegness, went to Littleworth for a period of four years, later to the horse department at King's Cross; a further move was made to Spalding, then to Parcels Dept, Lincoln, where he spent a number of years as vanman. He finally took up his position at Woodhall Spa in 1925, from which

Class K3 2-6-0 No. 61896 runs alongside the River Witham at Washingborough Junction with an excursion train from Skegness on 25 June 1955. *G. Flatters/A. Ludlam Collection.*

post he has retired. Mr Bebee carries with him the good wishes of all concerned'.

As with all railways in Britain, the Lincolnshire Loop was busy during both World Wars. It provided a diversionary route away from the heavily used Towns Line as well as continuing to be a vital source for foods for the rest of the country and servicemen overseas. The canning factory at Bardney had major contracts to supply canned goods for all the services, and Lincolnshire's ability to grow potatoes and vegetables, and the railway's ability to transport them, helped ensure that neither commodity ever needed to be rationed.

On at least one occasion during the conflict the line carried Royalty again. Railwayman Maurice Andrews remembered King George VI leaving from Woodhall Junction in 1944.

"I was just a lad, but I remember the Royal train in the platform. He came to visit the troops in Woodhall before they were dropped over Arnhem".

The Loop, along with the Horncastle branch and the New Line, were essential to the supply of fuel, bombs and ammunition to the air bases at Bardney, Woodhall Spa, Coningsby and East Kirkby. The trains also carried airmen to their bases, and troops to camps holding soldiers before the Arnhem landings. Railway wagons also carried the remains of airmen killed in action in aircraft that made it back to their bases. A lady porter at one station commented that it was very sad to see the remains of those young men being loaded into goods vans.

Michael Hubbard, the son of the station master at Woodhall Junction, saw some surprising locomotives passing through the station on diverted trains.

"The Flying Scotsman train came through one November on a diversion. It was pulled by an A3 – Woolwinder or Minoru – in black livery and very dirty as

Woodhall Junction station looking towards Lincoln in the 1950s. Note the impressive station nameboard and unusual Gent's toilet to the left of the waiting room. *D. Thompson/A. Ludlam Collection.*

A5 4-6-2T No. 69804 arrives at Bardney with a freight on 28 April 1959. *H. Casserley/A. Ludlam Collection.*

well. There was also a Southern Railway Schools class on a troop train."

Nationalisation after the war seemed to offer the prospect of a continuing role for the line, but the decline in passenger traffic saw the Horncastle branch lose that facility in 1955, one year short of its centenary. The driver of the last train, noting the large number of passengers commented that he would have liked to drop them all off in a field half-way back.

"They should have used it earlier, then we might not have lost it," he commented.

The writing was on the wall, though, or perhaps in Dr Beeching's notebook, in 1963, when his report on 'The Reshaping of British Railways' recommended total closure of the Loop to passenger traffic, with just Spalding to Peterborough retained for goods. The section

A fisherman waits on the platform at Dogdyke as Class B1 4-6-0 No. 61282 arrives with the 3.51pm Boston to Doncaster train on 22 October 1961. *A. Ludlam Collection.*

from Boston to Woodhall Junction closed that year, and most of the rest in October 1970.

The last passenger train saw very little in the way of public regret, and photographers who turned out to get a picture commented that 8.30pm on an October evening was not a good time for photography. A diesel multiple unit ran from Lincoln to Coningsby, but the lack of run-round facilities there meant it went on to Tumby Woodside and returned from there. Ironically, the name of Tumby Woodside, and that of Dogdyke were commemorated in the famous song, 'The Slow Train' by Flanders and Swann. However, a spirited local campaign got the passenger service from Spalding to Peterborough restored, with a delay of execution on two sections south of Lincoln. Lincoln to Woodhall Junction survived for another year to allow a goods train to continue to supply an agricultural merchant in Horncastle. The service was operated by a small diesel shunter with two wagons and a guards van, with the guard unlocking every crossing, allowing the train to pass through, and then relocking the gates.

John Cram, who worked the Horncastle pick-up goods in the 1960s, described the journey, and the unofficial activity that accompanied it.

"The train went to Bardney where the loco shunted the beet factory, then Morrell's canning factory before continuing on to Woodhall Junction and Horncastle, stopping along the way to check the snares that had been left by the lineside."

The run to Horncastle, and the supply of rabbits, ended in May 1971, but the line from Lincoln to Bardney remained in service until 1983 to allow coal to be supplied to the beet factory there.

Guard Froggatt with the Bardney Sugar Factory freight train on 23 May 1980. *M. Roughley/A. Ludlam Collection.*

Above:
The view from a Lincoln-bound DMU of Southrey station and signal box in 1970. *H. Johnston.*

Above:
A DMU calls at Woodhall Junction station on the final day. *Author's collection.*

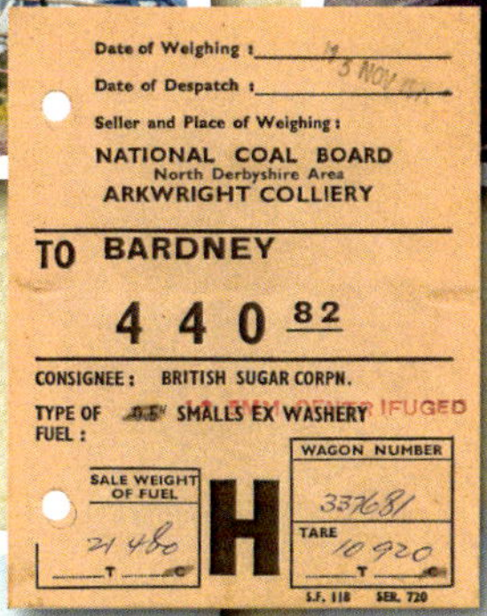

Above:
The Loop Line south of Boston just after the tracks had been lifted. *H. Johnston.*

An early postcard of Spalding station in GNR days.
Author's collection.

Above:
The remote Five Mile House station alongside the River Witham in October 1970. *B. Rose.*

Above:
The station House and signal box at Stixwould still exist today on the cycle route of the Water Rail Way from Boston to Lincoln.

Right:
The unusual cast iron gent's urinal from Woodhall Junction station, which can be seen in the photo on page 15, is now displayed at the Museum of Lincolnshire Life.

Below:
A present-day view of the elegant station buildings at Tattershall.

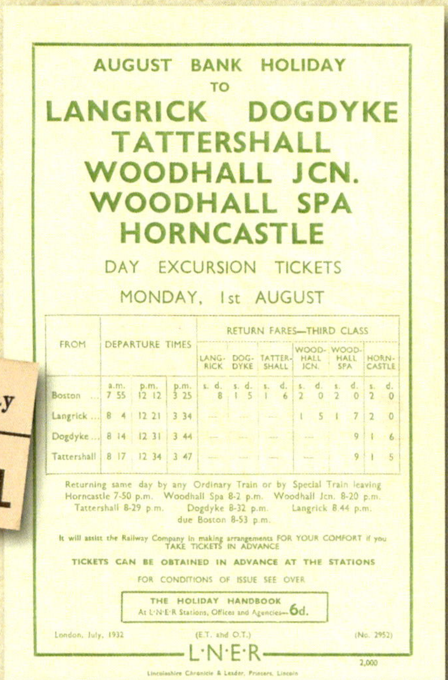

AUGUST BANK HOLIDAY
TO
LANGRICK DOGDYKE
TATTERSHALL
WOODHALL JCN.
WOODHALL SPA
HORNCASTLE

DAY EXCURSION TICKETS

MONDAY, 1st AUGUST

FROM	DEPARTURE TIMES			RETURN FARES—THIRD CLASS					
				LANG-RICK	DOG-DYKE	TATTER-SHALL	WOOD-HALL JCN.	WOOD-HALL SPA	HORN-CASTLE
	a.m.	p.m.	p.m.	s. d.	s. d.	s. d.	s. d.	s. d.	s. d.
Boston ...	7 55	12 12	3 25	8	1 5	1 6	2 0	2 0	2 0
Langrick ...	8 4	12 21	3 34	—	—	—	1 5	1 7	2 0
Dogdyke ...	8 14	12 31	3 44	—	—	—	—	9	1 6
Tattershall	8 17	12 34	3 47	—	—	—	—	9	1 5

Returning same day by any Ordinary Train or by Special Train leaving Horncastle 7-50 p.m. Woodhall Spa 8-2 p.m. Woodhall Jcn. 8-20 p.m. Tattershall 8-29 p.m. Dogdyke 8-32 p.m. Langrick 8.44 p.m. due Boston 8-53 p.m.

It will assist the Railway Company in making arrangements FOR YOUR COMFORT if you TAKE TICKETS IN ADVANCE

TICKETS CAN BE OBTAINED IN ADVANCE AT THE STATIONS

FOR CONDITIONS OF ISSUE SEE OVER

THE HOLIDAY HANDBOOK
At L·N·E·R Stations, Offices and Agencies—6d.

London, July, 1932 (E.T. and O.T.) (No. 2952)

L·N·E·R

2,000

Lincolnshire Chronicle & Leader, Printers, Lincoln

The Horncastle Branch

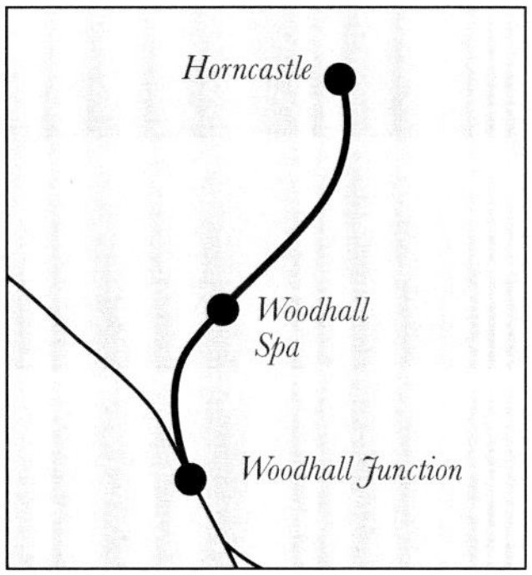

The Horncastle and Kirkstead Junction Railway was a private company promoted by the residents of Horncastle, an important market town on the edge of the Lincolnshire Wolds, with a population in the 1840s of about 25,000 people. They saw the benefits of railways to similar communities and financed their own branch line from the town to join the Great Northern Railway's Lincolnshire Loop Line, opened in 1848. The company was set up in 1853, and received Royal Assent in July 1854, despite opposition by the Horncastle Navigation Company, which had served the town and the village of Coningsby since completing the canalisation of the river Bain in 1803. The Navigation realised that the railway would take most of the traffic away from their waterway, but their protests fell on deaf ears. Suggestions that the railway might buy the Navigation, as the GN had bought the Witham, were not taken up, although the line lay alongside the canal for the final stretch into Horncastle.

The railway was very much a community operation. Its first chairman was local landowner Sir Henry

The Broadway, Woodhall Spa, onto which backed the station buildings. *A. Ludlam Collection.*

Dymoke, who carried the title of Queen's Champion, with another landowner, James Banks Stanhope MP, a descendant of the famous naturalist Joseph Banks, as one of his vice-chairman. The company raised £48,000 in capital, and another £13,000 in loans, and contractor Thomas Brassey, who had worked on the GN's route, built the line at a cost just under £60,000. An agreement was quickly reached with the Great Northern that the GN would operate the line in return for half of the earnings. It was opened to great fanfare in August 1855 just in time for the town's noted horse fair, which ensured a good cash flow for those first few days.

Other traffic carried in the early days included sheep, cattle and other livestock; large amounts of grain, local passengers and day trippers to London, thanks to the GN offering return trips to the city for 12/- (60p) first class and 6/- (30p) for less affluent travellers. Excursions were to prove a profitable sideline for many years, with those organised to Skegness by Jackson's, a local clothes shop, an annual occasion. In 1905 1,037 passengers were

Horncastle terminus. Class N5 0-6-2T No 69327 has marshalled the wagons for the 6.00 pm goods train and taken its place at the head of the 4.05 pm passenger train to Woodhall Junction. This view from the signal box shows the water tank and water column on the left.
J. Cupit/A. Ludlam Collection.

Woodhall Spa station looking toward Woodhall Junction in the 1950s. No doubt the signalman here was pretty fit, as he had to run from the signal box to open and close the crossing gates. *D. Thomson/A. Ludlam Collection.*

carried in two trains, one of 14 coaches and the other of 12, and the trip in July 1914 was accompanied by the Horncastle Silver Band, with a one shilling (5p) meat tea available in the Pavilion at Skegness for the trippers. Since the fare was only two shillings, that would have made for a good day out, although one cannot help but wonder how many of the young men on the train would have been back at the station a few weeks later to entrain for service in the Great War.

The Navigation owners tried to compete with the railway by reducing the fees paid by users, but the canal froze over that first winter of railway trading, and many users switched to the new service. Despite the weather, the price of coal, the most important commodity moved by either transport mode, fell by over 20% in the town during the winter of 1855/6. The canal remained in business for a number of years, particularly in the lower stretch as far as Coningsby, which did not get a rail connection for some time, but the company was closed down in 1889.

The line was just less than 8 miles long, with very few earthworks and a single bridge over its tracks close to the village of Martin. The terminus was at Horncastle, where an unusual goods layout saw a goods shed at right angles to the tracks served by a wagon turntable, with coal wagons continuing through the shed to the merchant's yard adjacent to the station. The tracks connected to the GN's Lincolnshire Loop just south of Kirkstead station. The junction ran towards Boston, resulting in trains having to reverse into the dedicated Horncastle bay platform at Kirkstead. A single station was initially planned for the village of Roughton, but that was changed to serve the similar-sized community of Woodhall Spa, where mineral waters had recently been discovered and a hotel and spa constructed. The change proved to be highly beneficial to the company, since much of the traffic in later years comprised large numbers of visitors coming to take the waters.

Table 53 WOODHALL JUNCTION, WOODHALL SPA, and HORNCASTLE

Miles	Week Days only	aft	mrn		mrn		aft	aft
	52 London (King's C.) dep	11F15	4 15	..	7 28	..	1 10	4 ‡5
—	Woodhall Junction dep	7a15	8 38	..	2 15	..	4 50	7 30
1½	Woodhall Spa	7 21	8 44	..	2 21	..	4 56	7 37
7½	Horncastle arr	7 37	8 53	..	2 37	..	5 5	7 46

Miles	Week Days only	mrn		mrn		aft		aft	
	Horncastle dep	7 55	..	9 0	..	1200	..	4 10	..
6	Woodhall Spa	8 5	..	9 10	..	1 0	..	4 20	..
7½	Woodhall Junction arr	8 10	..	9 15	..	1 5	..	4 25	..
130¼	52 London (King's C.) arr	12‡J30	..	1 15	..	5 55	..	10R2	..

a Mrn. ‡ Through Train, King's Cross to Boston. F Except Sat. nights, but applies on Sunday nights.
M Through Train from Boston, dep 6 57 aft (Table 52). J Restaurant Car, Grantham to King's Cross.
R Restaurant Car between King's Cross and Peterborough. ‡ Via Lincoln and Grantham.

Woodhall Junction to Horncastle Timetable from October 1942.

A significant boost to that traffic in the 1920s was the regular attendance by Queen Alexandra and her daughter Princess Victoria Louise, who came to visit Sir Archibald Weigall MP and his family at Petwood House, now the Petwood Hotel. To provide for such well-heeled travellers, the GNR ran a through carriage each day between King's Cross and Horncastle. The carriage left London attached to a train for Grimsby, but was taken off at Boston and added to the Horncastle train.

Not all travellers enjoyed such luxury. The local service in later years between Woodhall Junction and Horncastle was provided by a pair of ex-GNR steam railmotors which had had the engines removed and the two joined to create an articulated twin carriage which was pulled by one of a variety of small tank engines.

The company remained profitable throughout its existence, and was absorbed into the London and North Eastern Railway at the Grouping in 1923, and the Eastern Region of British Railways at nationalisation. The general decline in railway traffic saw passenger services end in 1955, with the final train hauled by an ex-Great Central 4-6-2 tank locomotive with twice the

Class A5 4-6-2T No 69804 of Lincoln shed stands in the bay platform at Woodhall Junction with a passenger train for Horncastle. Built for the GCR in May 1911, No 69804 was withdrawn in April 1958.

Class J6 0-6-0 No 64199 with a Railway Correspondence and Travel Society Special at Horncastle on 16 May 1954. The photo was taken from the signal box and shows the station area and the coal drops on the right. *Real Photographs Co. /A. Ludlam Collection.*

normal number of coaches carrying travellers seeking nostalgic memories or a sense of occasion.

Goods traffic continued for a further 16 years, including a period after closure of the Loop Line, when a train of one or two wagons ran to an agricultural merchant in Horncastle. The line closed completely in 1971, but only after Mr Newton Loynes, an employee of the National Farmers Union in Woodhall, had secured the final passenger ticket for a trip with the guard in his van.

For more information on this branch see the companion volume in this series Branch Lines of East Lincolnshire Volume Two Woodhall Junction to Horncastle, by A. J. Ludlam LWRS 2015.

Right: D4075 with a brake van crosses the main road in Woodhall Spa in 1970. *D. Enefer.*

James Andrew Webster (on left of picture with adze), GNR carpenter at Woodhall Spa with a new set of crossing gates which he, and the gang with him, had just installed in the village. *Author's Collection.*

THE HORNCASTLE RAILWAY.

DIVIDEND DECLARED 22nd MARCH, 1916.

Madam, *Horncastle, 22nd March, 1916.*

I beg to annex a Draft, No. 72 *, the balance of the Dividend on your shares in this Railway, for the year ending 31st December, 1915, after deducting the Interim Dividend paid 22nd September last, viz :*

	£ s. d.	£ s. d.
*.........*35*....Shares at 6/- per share*	10–10.0	
Less Income Tax at 3/3 per £	1.14.1	8.15.11

I am, Madam,
Your obedient Servant,
H. TWEED
Secretary.

I hereby certify that the Income Tax deducted from the amount of this Warrant has been, or will be, paid over by the said Company to the proper Officer for the receipt of Taxes.
H. TWEED, Secretary.

Miss S. E. Fletcher –

The New Line

Unlike most of the earlier railways in Lincolnshire, the New Line was promoted and built by the Great Northern Railway, rather than a locally promoted line run by the larger company. Its main purpose was to shorten the 'slow and irritating journey' passengers experienced travelling between Lincoln and the Lincolnshire Coast resorts, particularly Skegness, where local businesses had been agitating for better services from its important East Midlands and West Yorkshire markets. Some had been backing proposals for lines that would have challenged the GN's near monopoly in East and Central Lincolnshire, so a desire to pre-empt any such plans would certainly have played a part. The proposal was passed by Parliament in December 1911 as the Kirkstead and Little Steeping Railway, but the route was universally known as 'The New Line'.

The line was approved under legislation designed to facilitate the quick and easy construction of light railways, but was built to full main line standards, and may have adopted the light railway approach to reduce

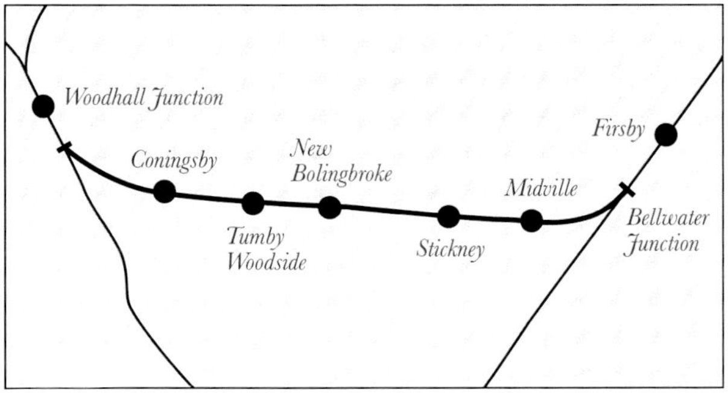

Building works on the New Line near Coningsby was interrupted by flooding. *H. Rundell/A. Ludlam Collection.*

the time and costs of a full Parliamentary approach. The engineer for the line was Alexander Ross, and H. Arnold and Son, from Doncaster, won the contract to build it at a price of just under £100,000 out of a total cost estimated at just over £200,000. Construction began in March 1912. An initial speed limit of 25mph, required for a light railway, was soon raised to 50mph for most of the route. Goods were carried from 1 June 1913 and passenger services commenced a month later, with four trains a day serving the stations between Lincoln and Skegness. The Engineer magazine noted that the time for a journey from Lincoln to Skegness fell from 3½ hours by the 'ordinary service' to an hour and 38 minutes, with the expresses covering the distance in less than 90 minutes. The daily service from Leeds to the resort was moved onto the new route, with through carriages from Manchester and Sheffield provided during the summer season. The Engineer was again pleased to see the improvements.

'This slow and irritating journey has become a thing of the past, for it is now possible, without change of carriage, for the holidaymaker to turn his back on the smoke and grime of Sheffield and, in a little time, find himself amid the pure atmosphere of Skegness.'

Services from Lincoln to Sutton on Sea and Mablethorpe also travelled over the New Line, with corresponding reductions in travel time.

The tracks left the Lincolnshire Loop at Coningsby Junction, a mile south of Kirkstead station, and joined the East Lincolnshire at Bellwater Junction, between

New Bolingbroke looking east in August 1970, with the later GNR signal box design and somersault signals. *P. Grey/A. Ludlam Collection.*

Eastville and Little Steeping. The route was almost entirely across flat fenland, requiring very little engineering work other than two road bridges and one over the River Bain at Coningsby plus a number of girder bridges over fen drains. Stations were built to a standard design at Coningsby, Tumby Woodside, New Bolingbroke, Stickney and Midville. Tumby Woodside and Midville were very small settlements, so the generous goods and passenger facilities provided could rarely have been used, although quantities of Lincolnshire's traditional crops of potatoes and sugar beet were regularly moved from all the stations.

One line of the double track was lifted during WW1 and sent to the Western Front as part of the British war effort. Unfortunately, as part of the German war effort, the ship carrying them was sunk in the English Channel and they never arrived at the Front. The double track was reinstated by 1923, in time for the grouping, which saw it become part of the London North Eastern Railway, which expanded its use for excursions, with additional services coming from the Midlands by way of Lincoln.

The outbreak of WW2 saw the facilities at Coningsby and Stickney used to a much greater extent when they became railheads for construction material, munitions and staff for the airfields at Coningsby and East Kirkby respectively. There was also a mock airfield at Hagnaby Lock designed to lure German aircraft away from the operational facilities elsewhere. The relative isolation of Midville made it a good place to store Pullman cars during the same war to remove them from the risk of damage at their usual base in London.

After that war, the line returned to its old role of conveying trippers to the seaside, but the decline in numbers travelling there by rail made it a candidate for the Beeching closures, although there was a small increase in numbers travelling to Firsby for connections to Boston after the line from Woodhall Junction to the town closed

The view from Bellwater Junction Signal Box in August 1970, with the New Line branching off to the right. *P. Grey/A. Ludlam Collection.*

in 1963. The stations became unstaffed in October 1963 and lost their goods facilities in March 1964. By 1970 the local service had been reduced to four trains a day from Lincoln to Firsby and three from the city to Tumby Woodside, a slightly surprising terminus given its small size, but one necessitated by the need to serve Coningsby and its RAF facilities, which did not have the track layout required for reversal.

The line was closed in October 1970 along with most of the other lines covered in this book. Most of the trackbed was rapidly reclaimed by farmers, with very little trace still to be found across the Fens, although many of the station buildings and crossing houses are still sitting in splendid isolation in the open countryside.

A DMU departs from Stickney in August 1970. *M. Hall/A. Ludlam Collection.*

Above: Midville station in 1970, Hobhole Drain is in the foreground, the level crossing, the ubiquitous booking office, signal box and waiting room beyond. *P. Grey/A. Ludlam Collection.*

Table 59 WOODHALL JUNCTION, CONINGSBY, and FIRSBY

Miles		Week Days mrn T		aft T		aft T		aft M		Sundays aft		
	52 Lincoln .... dep	9 17	..	1 5	..	5 47	..	10 45	..	10 15	..	..
—	Woodhall Junction.... dep	9 46	..	1 34	..	6 17	..	11 12	..	10 42	..	..
4½	Coningsby	9 54	..	1 42	..	6 25	..	11 20	..	10 50	..	..
6¾	Tumby Woodside..........	9 59	..	1 47	..	6 30	..	..	..	..	..	..
9	New Bolingbroke	10 4	..	1 52	..	6 35	..	..	..	..	..	..
11½	Stickney....................	10 9	..	1 57	..	6 40	..	..	..	..	..	..
14	Midville	1014	..	2 2	..	6 45	..	..	..	..	..	..
18	Little Steeping	1023	..	2 12	..	Aa	..	..	..	..	..	..
20½	Firsby .... arr	1028	..	2 17	..	6 57	..	..	..	..	..	..
29½	57 Skegness .... arr	1051	..	2 58	..	7 44	..	..	..	..	..	..

Miles		Week Days mrn T			aft T			aft T		Sundays		
	57 Skegness............ dep	7 50	..	..	1220	..	..	4 0	..	..	..	..
—	Firsby .... dep	8 30	..	..	1255	..	..	4 41	..	..	..	..
2½	Little Steeping	8 35	..	..	1 A0	..	..	4 46	..	..	..	..
6½	Midville	8 43	..	..	..	..	..	4 53	..	..	..	..
9	Stickney	8 48	..	..	1 11	..	..	4 58	..	..	..	..
11½	New Bolingbroke..........	8 53	..	..	1 16	..	..	5 3	..	..	..	..
13¾	Tumby Woodside..........	8 58	..	..	1A21	..	..	5 8	..	..	..	..
16	Coningsby	9 3	..	..	1 26	..	..	5 13	..	..	..	..
20½	Woodhall Junction ... arr	9 11	..	..	1 34	..	..	5 21	..	..	..	..
35¾	52 Lincoln .... arr	9 54	..	..	2 3	..	..	5 54	..	..	..	..

A Stops when required. Aa Stops when required to set down. M Mons., Fris., and Sats. T Through Trains between Lincoln and Skegness.

For **LOCAL TRAINS** between Little Steeping and Firsby, see Table 55.

Woodhall Junction, Coningsby and Firsby Timetable from October 1942.

Above:
A DMU leaving Coningsby on route to Lincoln in 1970. *H. Johnston.*

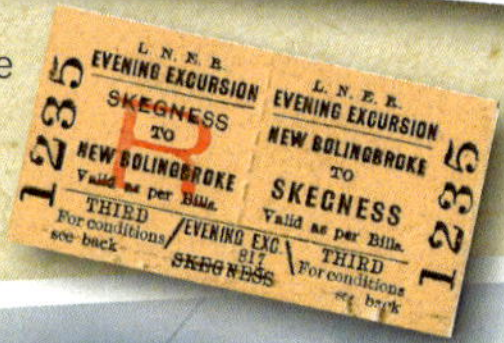

Above:
An ornate platform lamp at Tumby Woodside station. *P. Loftis.*

Above: New Bolingbroke station booking office now functions as an antique shop named the 'Junktion'.

Left: This present-day view at Midville looking west shows the remains of the bridge in the photo on page 29, which carried the railway over Hobhole drain.

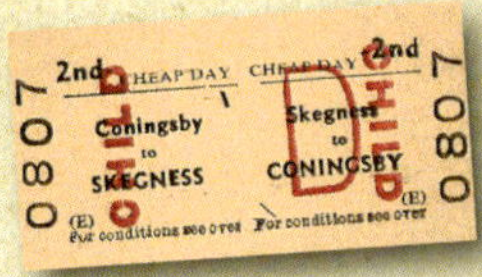

The East Lincolnshire Railway

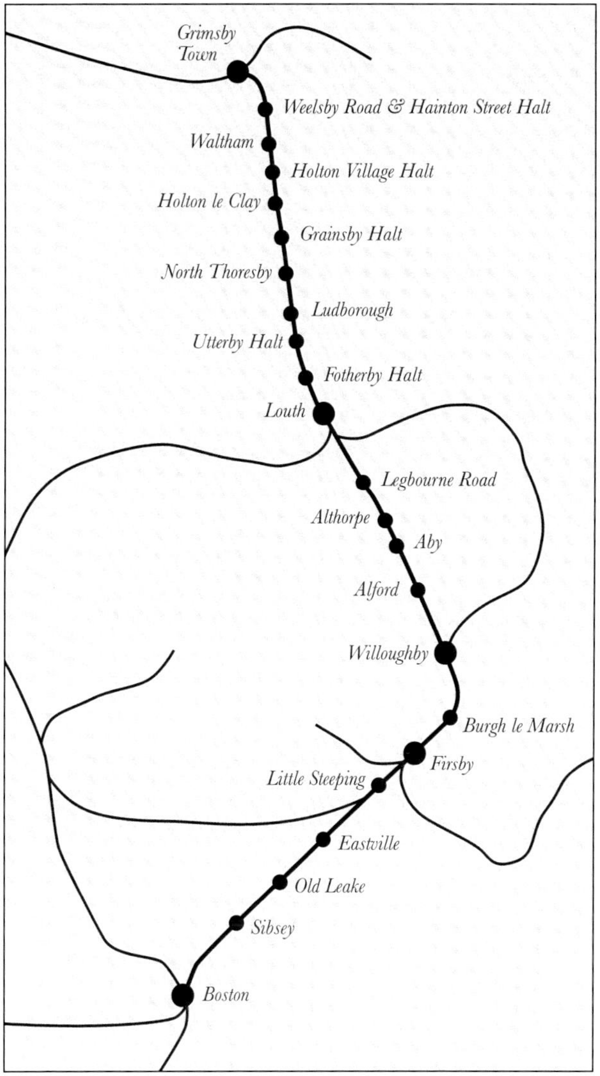

The East Lincolnshire Railway ran for 47 miles down the eastern side of Lincolnshire, connecting the port of Grimsby with The Great Northern Railway's Lincolnshire Loop Line at Boston. The line was double track throughout, and boasted two of the longest stretches of straight, level track in Britain, having been built mostly over the reclaimed lands of the Lincolnshire Fens and Marsh. The company worked closely with the Great Northern from the early planning stages, culminating in simultaneous passage through Parliament in June 1846. Two directors served on both boards throughout the early stages of the Bills and both lines received substantial local support. The East Lincolnshire may have had more visible local backers, including the Earl of Yarborough, the Earl of Ancaster, Lord Worsley and five county MPs, than the GNR, with its ambitions beyond the county boundaries, but many local investors backed both enterprises.

In its prospectus, the ELR claimed that their line would establish 'a communication by railways along the coast of an important maritime district', offering 'cheap and ready access to the markets of London and Yorkshire'. This would be of particular benefit to graziers and cattle feeders on the Marsh, and wool producers on the Wolds, who could avoid the 'tedious and expensive' carriage by cart, barge and boat then required. The promoters also expected the line to win a share of the growing fish traffic leaving from the expanding town of Grimsby, where another company,

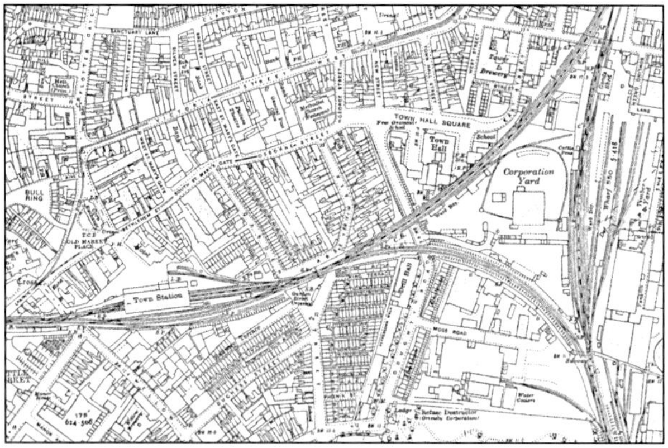

As this map shows, Grimsby Town station was quite severly restricted by busy level crossings at both ends. The East Lincolnshire line runs off at the bottom right, the line to the docks and Cleethorpes runs in the opposite direction.

the Manchester, Sheffield and Lincolnshire, had invested heavily in the dock facilities, and were opening a new line to serve the industrial cities of the north.

In addition to the benefits of outgoing trade, 'manufactured goods and articles of merchandise' would be brought into the towns served by the line, as well as the expected cheaper coal and building materials.

Throughout its existence, up to the railway grouping of 1923, when it became part of the London and North Eastern Railway, the ELR remained independent and profitable through its connection with the GN, which leased and operated it for the whole time.

Along its route, the company had substantial covered stations in the market towns of Louth, Alford and Boston. Between Grimsby and Louth it served stations at Waltham, Holton-le-Clay, North Thoresby and Ludborough. From 1905 there were also simple halts with short, low platforms at Hainton St, Weelsby Road, Holton Village, Grainsby, Utterby and Fotherby. Utterby and Fotherby had opened briefly in the early history of the line, but had closed by 1872, before reopening, along with new halts at the others, to be served by a steam railmotor service between Louth and Grimsby.

At Louth one branch, the Louth and East Coast Railway, left the main line to serve the farming communities on the Lincolnshire Marsh and the coastal village of Mablethorpe, while another, the Louth and Lincoln Railway, crossed the Wolds to meet the Lincolnshire loop at Bardney.

Heading south from Louth the line served Legbourne Road, Authorpe and Aby and Claythorpe before arriving at Alford. Next was Willoughby, the junction for another branch to the sea, the Sutton and Willoughby Railway, serving Sutton on Sea, followed by Burgh le Marsh and the imposing structure at Firsby. This was a remarkably large station for a very small village, although it later served as the junction for the branches to Skegness, the Wainfleet and Firsby Railway, and Spilsby, the Spilsby and Firsby Railway. Firsby, like Louth, was originally served by a large wooden goods shed, but both structures were destroyed by a storm in 1860 and replaced by the more common brick and slate structures.

Beyond Firsby, on the approach to Boston, stations served Little Steeping, Eastville, Old Leake – originally Hobhole after the adjacent drain - and Sibsey before joining the Lincolnshire Loop just before the shared bridge over the Grand Sluice close to the town station. The ELR had originally planned to have its own station in the town, rather closer to the docks than that finally jointly decided by the two companies, although a branch

A beautiful scene at the southern end of Alford station in Great Northern Railway days showing the overall roof. The southbound train of 6-wheeler carriages is drawn by a GNR 2-2-2 engine No. 266. *Stewart Neil Collection.*

Weelsby Road level-crossing and halt. The crossing was replaced by a subway in 1933. *A. Ludlam Collection.*

was laid into the docks, and continues to serve them.

Like the ELR itself, all the branches served from stations on the line were leased or owned by the GNR and were operated by that company. All closed, apart from Skegness, at or before the October 1970 closure of most of the East Lincolnshire line. The only parts of that line still in service are the stretch from Boston to just short of Firsby, though not making use of the station there, nor any of the stations previously served, and a section north of Louth owned and operated by the Lincolnshire Wolds Railway, which plans to put more back into use in the future.

Construction and Operation

Once Parliamentary approval had been secured, building began in several places – in fact 'excavation and levelling' near Grimsby had already been noted by the Lincoln and Stamford Mercury newspaper before formal contracts had been announced. By January 1846 work was taking place on a number of sites in the area, with temporary rails laid and 60-70 men employed, including brick makers preparing materials for bridges and culverts. There was local shock and horror that some employees were working on a Sunday, and one local paper noted approvingly that the contractor had been fined for this misdemeanour.

The urgency at the northern end was partly due to a need to match the opening times of part of the Manchester, Sheffield and Lincolnshire, which owned the station in Grimsby that the East Lincolnshire was going to use. The ELR had planned to serve the ferries across the Humber, from New Holland to Hull, using MS&L tracks from Grimsby to New Holland. The MS&L would also have running rights over the ELR as far as Louth. The two sections of track concerned were the first to be opened by the companies, on 1 March 1848, although special trains carrying the directors and others were run in both directions the previous day, with pleasantries and hospitality exchanged as they crossed at Grimsby.

This amicable situation lasted for about a year before an argument about the GN's station in London caused relations to sour. The MS&L stopped GN trains from using their station at Grimsby or their tracks through to the ferries. An occasional GN train did get access, but the MS&L, who owned the ferries, sent the last one off early to prevent the connection being made. The passengers spent the night on the train. The dispute was not settled until 1851 when it was agreed that the GN could use Grimsby, but not the lines to the ferry, and the

MS&L lost their rights for traffic to Louth.

In the meantime, the rest of the ELR had opened in stages. 20 miles of track from Louth to Firsby opened on the 1 September 1848, celebrated by the running of six trains from Firsby to Grimsby on the opening day. With the 14 mile link through to Boston completed by 1 October 1848, the company joined the ELR in its opening celebrations on the 17th referred to earlier, which marked the opening of the Lincolnshire Loop, allowing connections through to Peterborough. Through trains to London and the south became possible a few months later with the opening of the GN line to King's Cross.

Construction had presented few technical problems. The flat lands that were crossed required very few major engineering works, although the wet nature of the land did create some problems. John Waring and Son, from Rotherham, had won the contract to build the entire line, and did complete the section from Grimsby to Louth, although two timber bridges they installed had to be

Ludborough station, showing the station house and the low platform, used by the Grimsby-Louth railmotor trains. *A. Ludlam Collection.*

replaced when their foundations sank into the boggy soil.

Warings chose not to complete their contract for the longer section between Louth and Boston, which was taken over by the well-known railway builders, Peto and Betts. The partnership had been formed during the building of the Lincolnshire lines, and helped them acquire the expertise that later allowed them to build the Grand Trunk Railway in Canada and the Grand Crimean Central Railway as well as many other lines in the UK and abroad.

What they would not have got in Lincolnshire was experience in large engineering works. Nothing here matched the requirements of the 2-mile Victoria Bridge in Canada, which they built over the St Lawrence River on 24 ice-breaking piers. On the ELR they constructed a single two-arch brick viaduct, one large brick bridge and installed a ninety-foot steel girder bridge over the large Maud Foster Drain. Other drains on what was often reclaimed marsh or fen land did need to be crossed, but low embankments and viaducts and large numbers of culverts and smaller bridges did not require the line to rise above the land surface very often. What the

A class B1 4-6-0 leaves Grimsby Town station with a train for Cleethorpes while another member of the class waits to depart platform 2 with a London bound train, on 30 September 1959. Note Garden Street signal box and the impressive gantry of signals with the East Lincolnshire line diverging off to the right. *A. C. Ingram/A. Ludlam Collection.*

company might have become expert at was the installation of level crossings. There were 95 of them between Boston and Louth, a number that proved to be a fatal problem in later years.

They may also have gained experience in handling civil disturbances. Fights between workers or between workers and locals were not uncommon, often spurred by intake of 'the demon drink'. Local celebrations, such as annual 'feasts', common in Lincolnshire villages at the time, could provide an opportunity for larger scale mayhem. The North Thoresby Feast of 1847 saw 'a great number of farmers' servants' do battle with 'a considerable number of workmen on the East Lincolnshire Railway'. The Lincolnshire Chronicle described it as 'a serious affray', causing 'a most fearful disturbance'. Fortunately, despite 'Stakes and bludgeons' being used, no deaths occurred. The paper also reported no charges had been brought because 'the night being dark prevented the constabulary from recognising friend from foe'.

Open for business

As soon as a full service could be operated, the line proved a success. One local paper claimed that the receipts of over £60,000 in the first two weeks was twice the operating costs, a situation that The Railway Chronicle felt was worthy of comment.

"The shareholders of the Great Northern are to be congratulated on the wise management of their affairs, so as to give them at so early a period and so small a cost a beneficial return on the money already spent. By it, a

Burgh-le-Marsh station taken from Skegness Road, with the full complement of the station and yard staff. The goods shed stands beyond the station platform. *A. Ludlam Collection.*

large district, largely cut off from the benefits of railway communication, is now opened up and one of the producing and agricultural districts of England is brought into connexion with the metropolis, and with the consuming districts which will henceforth be the most profitable market for its produce."

Rather unusually for railways promoted in Lincolnshire, the ELR's predictions of its goods traffic and the benefits to the community turned out to be generally correct. Cattle were moved in large numbers both in and out of the areas served. A notable increase was in animals being brought onto the Marsh to be 'finished' – fattened for slaughter – before being sold, particularly at Louth, for slaughter locally or taken by train for killing elsewhere. Grain and potatoes were staples of the line, along with sugar beet once local processing factories opened in the 1920s. Valuable fertiliser was brought in, often in the shape of horse manure cleared from the streets and stables of the big cities, where horse-drawn transport was still the norm. The same horses also needed a regular supply of hay and straw which could both be provided by farmers in the area. Specialist growers around Aby shipped out wagons loaded with watercress, and agricultural lime came from quarries on the Wolds. Water for growing watercress needs to be very clean, which may be one of the reasons that the area was chosen to supply fresh water to Lincoln during a typhoid epidemic in 1905. The water was carried in old locomotive tenders, so the purity may have been rather reduced by the time it arrived, but a little rust was considered less of a problem than the disease.

The promoters were also right about the fish. Grimsby became the most important fishing port in the country, a process accelerated by the GN persuading fishermen from the south coast to move into the new docks in the town. The rate of growth can be seen from the fact that 450 tons of fish left the port in 1854, before much of the expansion had taken place, compared to over 130,000 tons by 1900.

WD 2-8-0 No. 90159 passing through Eastville station in July 1961. *A. Ludlam Collection.*

The increase had been accelerated by the development of fish and chips as a major food stuff in the industrial cities. Much of that trade was handled by the MS&L, which had become the Great Central in 1897, but the GN developed a speciality of fast fish trains to London. These trains, normally two a day, were treated with the same priority as express passenger services, with motive power to match. One of Stirling's splendid Singles was noted on a fish train in the early 1900s, and new Britannia Class Pacifics and 9F 2-10-0 heavy goods were among the final steam locos to power the trains. Fast was a fair description of the service, which was supposedly restricted to a maximum of 45 wagons travelling at 60mph, although one commentator noted the regular passage of up to 100 wagons travelling at what seemed to be speeds well in excess of the limit. It was also fragrant – Joan Hewson said the smell of fish spread far and wide as the train sped by.

The straight, level lines allowed high speeds to be achieved even by older and smaller engines, so as the single-wheelers and Atlantics became outdated on the expresses of the Towns Line, now the East Coast Main line, they found Lincolnshire's lines, and the ELR in particular, very appropriate.

Fireman Brian Bell was very happy to have worked the line in later years.

An Immingham-based class B1 4-6-0 No 61130 comes to a stand alongside Louth South signal box, with a morning Cleethorpes-King's Cross passenger train in the early 1960s. *B. G. Tweed/A. Ludlam Collection.*

"The East Lincs was a smashing route because it was very, very flat and almost dead straight, which makes a big difference to a locomotive."

On one occasion, though, the locomotive proved up to the job, but the crew were found lacking. During the 1926 General Strike a strike-breaking clergyman and two students drove a fish train from Grimsby to Boston. They took seven hours, rather than the usual less than two, and demolished every crossing gate along the way.

From the 1930s, iron ore was moved along the ELR from mines near Grantham to the steelworks at Scunthorpe. Although this was a rather round-about route, it avoided blocking the main line through Newark with slow moving goods.

A work-stained class B1 4-6-0 No 61168 stands at platform 2 at Grimsby Town with a London-bound passenger train in 1960. The white smokebox door straps were a feature of Immingham engines. *R. Conway/A. Ludlam Collection.*

Passenger traffic was always expected to be important to the ELR, and it proved to be so, even if the hoped-for business to Yorkshire and the north by way of the Humber Ferries never developed to the extent predicted. The real success was in carrying traffic that had not been anticipated; the millions of trippers and holiday-makers who used the line to get to the seaside at Skegness, Sutton, Mablethorpe and even onto MS&L/GC territory at Cleethorpes.

Before the railways arrived, these communities had been, at best, coastal villages with a trickle of visitors arriving on foot or by horse. Skegness, in 1842, had a population of less than 200, and its two small hotels probably did more business with the little harbour than it did with holiday makers. Mablethorpe and Sutton – then known as the less visitor-inclined Sutton on the Marsh – could only boast about 300 residents each by the 1850s. The railways turned the trickle of visitors into a flood. Trains arrived in Skegness in 1873, Mablethorpe in 1877 and Sutton on Sea in 1886. The line to Sutton was extended to Mablethorpe in 1888, creating a loop of track that ran from Louth to Willoughby, each on the ELR, passing through both towns. Despite the fact that the Mablethorpe line was originally promoted, with two unbuilt additional branches, as a line to serve the farming community, and Skegness was an extension of a route built to serve the port of Wainfleet, traffic on all the lines became dominated by leisure travellers.

Skegness led the way, with developments to attract visitors spearheaded by the Earl of Scarbrough, who owned most of the town. He laid out a new town, invested heavily in pleasure gardens, a pier, and some very necessary drainage works. In return he received a farthing, about 1/10 p, from the railway for each passenger arriving by train. That would have given the Earl an additional income of about £100 in 1880, when over 100,000 visited the town. A local paper report claimed that so many trippers turned up on August Bank Holiday 1882 that they stripped the town of anything available to eat or drink leaving it 'as bare of nutriments as was Egypt after the visitation of the locusts'.

Numbers peaked in the 1930s, with Skegness averaging over 700,000 a year and Mablethorpe seeing 166,000 arrive in 1936, and every one of them contributed to the finances of the London and North Eastern Railway, which had absorbed the ELR and the branches. A large proportion were carried on excursions, including some from London to Skegness that only allowed for three hours in the town, but many used the regular services. These had risen from six a day each way in 1849 to eight a day in the 1920s. There were also trains which only ran between Grimsby and Louth, although some continued onto the branch to Mablethorpe. At peak goods traffic times, such as the potato season, as many as seven goods trains a day ran, including the two fast fish trains.

Some trains were so long that they had to call twice at some stations with relatively short platforms. James Milne remembered passengers rushing towards the front of the train when it first stopped, afraid that they had missed their chance to alight, only to find themselves still unable to get off when the train moved forward to allow rear passengers to leave.

Outings did not have to be long-haul, or just to the seaside. Robert Baglin needed the trains to follow his favourite football team – Grimsby Town, The Mariners.

"I remember alighting at Grimsby Town station and walking all the way to Cleethorpes as my parents couldn't afford the extra cost, so had to walk in all weathers there and back to the station for the return journey home after the match".

The railway station at Louth was also Robert's childhood play area, doing things he would almost certainly be prevented from doing today.

"My brother and I played at Louth station watching the trains and riding on the Keddington Road level crossing gates several times a day as they were operated, which

Table 55 BOSTON, FIRSBY, WILLOUGHBY, LOUTH, and GRIMSBY TOWN

Miles from Boston		Week Days													Suns	
		aft	mrn	mrn	mrn	mrn (From Lincoln (Table 59))	mrn	mrn	aft (From Lincoln (Table 59))	aft	aft	T aft	aft	aft	mrn	aft
	52 London (King'sC.) dep	11H15	..	..	4 15		..	7 23		1 10	..	4 5	..	5R50	10 10	6 5
	52 Peterboro (North) "	3a0	..	..	6 35		..	1054		3 0	..	5 57	..	7 50	1p35	8 0
	2 Leicester (Cen.). "	10L36	..	..	..		..	7K5		8 10	..	1P35	..	2 52	6Pa56	..
	54 Derby (Friargate) "	10H40	..	..	..		..	7 40		9 12	..	1P18	..	4 0	10P10	..
	54 Nottingham (Vic.) "	11H25	..	..	..		..	8 30		10 9	..	3P25	..	5 0	11P0	..
	54 Grantham "	1aP18	..	..	6 15		..	9 55		1258	..	5P7	..	6 48	12P41	6P46
—	Boston dep	4 2	..	..	7 48		..	1213		3 54	..	6 51	..	9 13	2 52	9 1
4¾	Sibsey	..	..	..	7 57		..	1223		4 3	..	..	..	9 22	3 1	..
6¼	Old Leake	..	..	..	8 1		..	1227		4 7	..	..	..	9S26	3 5	..
9¾	East Ville	..	..	..	8 8		..	1234		4 13	..	..	..	9 31	3 11	..
12¾	Little Steeping	..	..	..	8 15	1023	..	1241	2 12	4 20	..	..	..	9S39	..	..
15	Firsby arr	4 22	..	..	8 20	1028	..	1246	2 17	4 25	..	7 13	..	9Z41	3 20	9 23
24¼	57 Skegness arr	7 34	..	..	9 0	1051	..	1 22	2 58	5 9	..	7 44	..	10 16	4 1	9 59
—	Firsby dep	4 31	..	..	8 26	..	10 40	1252	Stop	4 30	..	7 20	..	9Z48	3 30	9 30
17	Burgh-le-Marsh	4 39	..	..	8 31	..	10 45	1257		4 35	..	7 25	..	9Z53	3 35	9 37
20¾	Willoughby arr	..	..	..	8 38	..	10 52	1 4	..	4 42	..	7 32	..	..	3 42	..
27¾	58 Sutton-on-Sea .. arr	8B19	..	..	9 8	..	11 8	2B20	..	5 25	..	8 6	..	..	..	..
30½	58 Mablethorpe .. "	8B12	..	..	9 14	..	11 14	2B13	..	5 32	..	8 12	..	..	..	..
—	Willoughby dep	..	..	..	8 43	..	10A55	1 9	..	4 45	5A12	7 34	7A55	..	3 52	..
23¼	Alford Town	4p53	..	..	8 50	..	..	1 16	..	4 52	..	7 40	..	10Z6	3 59	9 50
26¼	Aby, for Claythorpe	..	..	..	8 56	..	..	1 22	..	4 58	..	..	..	..	4 5	..
27½	Authorpe	..	..	..	9 0	..	..	1 26	..	..	..	..	..	..	4 9	..
31	Legbourne Road	..	..	..	9 7	..	..	1 33	..	..	..	..	..	..	..	..
33½	Louth arr	5 9	..	..	9 13	..	11A45	1 39	aft	5 10	6A3	7 56	8A40	10Z21	4 23	10 5
	Louth dep	5 17	6 30	7 42	9 17	..	12 0	1 42	4 14	5 15	6 8	7 59	8 45	10Z26	4 28	1012
36¼	Fotherby	..	..	7 48	..	..	12 6	..	4 20	..	6 14	..	..	..	..	..
38¼	Utterby	..	..	Aa	..	..	Aa	..	Aa	..	Aa	..	..	..	..	..
39	Ludborough	..	6 39	7 54	9 26	..	12 12	1 51	4 26	..	6 20	..	8 54	..	4 37	..
40½	North Thoresby	5 27	6 43	7 58	9 30	..	12 16	1 55	4 30	..	6 24	8 10	8 58	10Z38	4 41	1024
41½	Grainsby	..	..	..	..	..	..	..	..	..	..	..	..	..	..	..
42½	Holton-le-Clay	..	6 48	8 3	9 36	..	12 21	2 0	4 35	..	6 29	..	9 3	..	4 46	..
43½	Holton Village	..	6 51	8 6	9 39	..	12 24	2 3	4 38	..	6 32	..	9 6	..	..	..
44½	Waltham	..	6 55	8 10	9 45	..	12 28	2 7	4 42	..	6 36	..	9 10	..	4 51	..
46¾	Weelsby Road	..	..	..	..	..	..	..	..	..	..	..	..	..	..	..
47	Hainton Street	..	..	8 15	..	..	..	..	..	..	..	..	..	..	..	..
47½	Grimsby Town arr	5 39	7 2	8 18	9 51	..	12 34	2 13	4 49	5 34	6 42	8 23	9 16	10Z51	4 57	1037
50¾	68 Cleethorpes arr	6 10	7 26	8 36	1032	..	1 40	3 1	..	6 6	6 59	8 46	1018	..	6 J1	1059

	Week Days														Suns	
	mrn	mrn	mrn	U	aft	aft	aft	aft	aft	aft	aft	aft	aft	aft	mrn	aft
68 Cleethorpes dep	..	6 55	815	8 40	1225	..	1 10	2 35	..	3 28	5 22	6 35	6 50	..	9 0	4‡20
Grimsby Town dep	5 50	7 12	838	9 5	1 5	..	1 30	3 4	..	5 0	5 45	6 55	7 50	9 42	9 21	6V0
Hainton Street	..	..	..	..	..	..	..	..	..	..	..	..	..	..	Z	..
Weelsby Road	..	..	..	..	..	..	..	..	..	..	..	..	..	..	..	..
Waltham	5 56	7 19	845	..	1 12	..	..	3 11	..	5 6	5 51	7 1	7 57	9 48	9 28	..
Holton Village	..	..	849	..	1 16	..	..	Zz	..	..	5 55	7 5	..	9 52	..	..
Holton le-Clay	6 2	..	852	..	1 19	..	..	3 18	..	..	5 58	7 7	..	9 55	9 34	..
Grainsby	..	..	..	..	..	..	..	..	..	..	..	..	..	..	..	..
North Thoresby	6 7	7 27	857	9 17	1 24	..	..	3 23	..	5 13	6 3	7 13	8 4	10 0	9 39	6 12
Ludborough	6 11	7 31	9 1	..	1 28	..	..	3 27	..	..	6 7	7 17	..	10 4	9 43	..
Utterby	..	..	9 4	..	Aa	..	..	..	..	..	..	7 20	..	Aa	..	..
Fotherby	..	..	9 9	..	1 35	..	..	..	..	..	..	7 25	..	Rr	..	..
Louth arr	6 20	7 40	915	9 29	1 41	..	1 50	3 36	..	5 25	6 16	7 31	8 16	1013	9 52	6 24
Louth dep	6 25	7A44	..	9 33	Stop	..	1 52	3 40	..	5 29	6A20	..	8 21	..	9 55	6 28
Legbourne Road	6 30	..	..	..	Stop	..	..	3 45	..	..	..	..	..	..	..	..
Authorpe	6 36	..	..	..	..	..	..	3 52	..	5 37	..	..	..	..	10 4	..
Aby for Claythorpe	6 39	..	..	..	..	..	..	3 56	..	..	..	..	..	..	10 8	..
Alford Town	6 47	..	..	9 49	..	..	2 9	4 3	..	5 47	..	..	8 39	..	1016	6 43
Willoughby arr	6 52	8A34	..	9 54	..	..	2 14	4 8	..	5 52	7A19	..	8 44	..	1021	6 48
58 Mablethorpe dep	..	Stop	..	9 20	..	..	11F16	3 45	..	4 45	..	..	7 0	..	..	..
58 Sutton-on-Sea "	..		..	9 28	mrn	..	11B9	3 52	..	4 51	..	..	7 7	..	..	..
Willoughby dep	6 54	..	..	9 56	10 5	..	2 16	4 19	..	5 57	..	..	8 46	..	1031	6 50
Burgh-le-Marsh	7 1	..	..	..	1013	..	2 24	4 26	..	6 4	..	..	8 54	..	1038	..
Firsby arr	7 5	mrn	..	10 6	1017	..	2 28	4 30	..	6 8	..	..	8 59	..	1042	6 59
57 Skegness dep	6 35	7 50	..	9 33	..	1221	2 0	[illegible]	4 0	5 30	..	..	8 25	..	1015	6 30
Firsby dep	7 8	8 30	..	1013	..	1255	2 34	4 36	4 41	6 14	..	..	9 5	..	1052	7 1
Little Steeping	7 13	8 35	..	..	..	Aa	..	4 41	4 46	..	..	..	..	..	..	..
East Ville	7 20	To Lincoln (Table 59)	..	..	..	To Lincoln (Table 59)	..	4 48	To Lincoln (Table 59)	..	..	..	..	..	11 4	..
Old Leake	7 26		..	..	..		..	4 54		..	..	..	..	..	1111	..
Sibsey	7 30		..	..	..		..	4 59		..	..	..	..	..	1117	..
Boston arr	7 39		..	1035	..		2 56	5 12		6 36	..	..	9 27	..	1127	7 23
54 Grantham arr	9 18		..	1158	..		6P13	7 5		..	..	..	1043	..	3P30	10P35
54 Nottingham (Vic.) "	11 26		..	1 47	..		7P20	8 57		..	..	..	..	..	7P39	..
54 Derby (Friargate) "	12U48		..	2 38	..		..	9 54		..	..	..	..	..	..	..
2 Leicester (Cen.) "	12p54		..	4 18	..		8T33	10 4		..	..	..	..	..	8P37	..
52 Peterboro (North) "	8a38		..	1132	..		3 55	6 37		7 44	..	..	1028	..	1243	8 21
52 London (King's C.) "	10 52		..	1 15	..		5 55	..		10R2	..	..	2a40	..	2 36	10 18

NOTES

A Via Mablethorpe
Aa Stops when required. Passengers wishing to alight must inform Guard at the preceding *stopping* station.
a Morn
B Via Louth
H Via Peterborough. Except Sat. nights Dep Derby 10 5 and Nottingham 10 45 aft on Sundays
J Arr 5 33 aft from 29th Nov. to 27th Dec., 1942 inclusive
K Leicester (Belgrave Road). Passengers can depart Leicester (Central) at 6 56 mrn
L Via Peterborough. Except Sat. nights. Dep 6 54 aft on Suns
F Except. Sats. applies also on Sundays
P Via Peterborough
p Aft
R Restaurant Car between King's Cross and Peterborough
Rr Calls when required to set down on notice being given at Grimsby Town
S Saturdays only
T Through Train King's Cross to Cleethorpes
T Via Peterborough. Arr 9 12 aft on Sats. Passengers can arr. Leicester (Belgrave Road) 8 50 aft daily
U Through Train Cleethorpes to King's Cross
U Arr 12 58 aft Sats.
V Through Train, Grimsby to King's Cross
y Arr 5 mins *earlier*
Z Through Train, Cleethorpes to King's Cross
Z 3 mins later Sats.
Zz Calls on Fridays only at 3 15 aft when required Passengers wishing to alight must inform Guard at preceding *stopping* station

‡ Dep 5 5 aft on 11th and 18th Oct., 1942, and from 21st Feb. to 4th April, 1943 inclusive

For **OTHER TRAINS** between Willoughby and Louth, see Table 58

Boston to Grimsby Timetable from October 1942.

Britannia 4-6-2 70040 'Clive of India' at East Lincs Junction, Boston, with the morning Cleethorpes to King's Cross express on 18 June 1962. *G. Brown Collection.*

obviously wouldn't be allowed today but nobody cared in those days, as we roamed around at will. The station and subway were our playground. Happy memories of a great childhood and of that section of the line."

WW1 caused a reduction in the seaside traffic, but that was partly made up by large numbers of troops arriving at training camps in the area or for military exercises. Goods traffic also increased, carrying supplies for the troops and helping support military operations and facilities around Grimsby, where many of the fishing boats were being used for mine-detecting and other naval support work.

WW2 saw a similar change of use, with many special trains to Skegness to serve the Navy's HMS Royal Arthur, which wasn't a ship, but Butlin's holiday camp, which had been requisitioned as a training facility. Construction material and workers for the airfield at Strubby were delivered to Aby station. Grimsby's trawlers were again taken into military service, carrying out anti-submarine and patrol purposes as well as for mine-sweeping. Immingham, just beyond the ELR, was a major military base, particularly after the invasion of Europe.

The line itself came under direct attack on several occasions when bombs were dropped on Louth and Alford stations. Nine people were killed in two of the raids, four of them railway staff and the rest civilians. An armoured train patrolled the line, staffed by Polish soldiers with anti-tank 'bazooka' rockets and machine guns, and equipped with 2 six-pounder guns, preparing for an attack over the Lincolnshire coast which fortunately never happened.

The war also caused the closure to passengers of one of the branches served by the ELR. Services were withdrawn to Spilsby on the outbreak of the war 'for the duration of hostilities' but never returned when it was over. The line, with just one intermediate station, had opened in 1868 with hopes of matching the commercial success of its neighbours Horncastle, on the other side of the Wolds, but never managed to achieve the same returns.

The end of the war saw a return to normal services, although the very bad winter of 1947 brought trains to a stop in several sections of the line. A trainload of people had to be accommodated by the station master and staff at North Thoresby and feedstuffs had to be delivered by a local farmer to cattle stranded in a train on the line. Joan Hewson caught one of the last trains from London to Louth not to be held up, but she remembered that it was a very cold journey with a slightly spooky fellow traveller.

"The guard's van had a stove in it, so I travelled with the guard, but the van also carried a coffin. I don't know if it was occupied!"

1947 was also the year in which British Railways took control of the line, along with all other railways in the country. Investment was provided to help the railways recover from war-time damage and wear and tear, and the 1950s saw traffic increasing again. Charles Sharpe described Boston station on a Saturday night in the 50s.

"Between 8 and 9.30 it was a heaving mass of country people who had been shopping in the town or had been to the pictures, and were on the way home. The 8.27 to Grimsby made special stops on Saturdays at the stations between Boston and Firsby. The Grimsby mail came in and left and the Grantham mail came out of the sidings to be loaded and depart - both of those made extra stops along the way. It was a busy working station."

North Thoresby, looking towards Grimsby. *A. Ludlam Collection.*

The good times also returned for Lincolnshire's seaside resorts. Mablethorpe never quite got back to its 1936 total of 166,000 train travellers, but the 136,000 in 1959 was still a very satisfying figure for the town, and for the small boys with home-made trolleys who Maureen Monk remembered would take their luggage to a hotel or boarding house for half a crown (12.5p).

The numbers may have been helped that year by the arrival in Louth of Bertram Mills Circus, all of which arrived by train. Jim Triffitt was impressed by one of the attractions.

"The elephants were unloaded and walked through the town to Newmarket and on to where the Circus was held. What a sight that was!"

Excursions could also be good for the train crew. Denis Lowe was the fireman with driver Fred Marsh on a special trip from Nottingham to Sutton and Mablethorpe. He had an easy job firing a recently serviced K2 2-6-0 on the flat lines, and an even easier time in the town.

"On a lovely hot summer's day, after a nice fish and chip lunch, Fred and I spent the afternoon looking around the town and relaxing on the beach until it was time for the return journey to Nottingham. Happy days!"

The day was certainly happy for one crew. They took their families with them and, according to Percy Carter, overdid the holiday atmosphere.

"They spent the day in the boozer, and weren't fit to take the train back".

Firsby station box with Duty Signalman Moore at the helm. His colleague is turning the wheel to open the gates to road traffic. The illuminated track diagram and block bell shelf can seen above the frame. *G. Brown Collection.*

What the increase in rail travel masked was the numbers arriving by bus or private car, which rapidly became the dominant modes of transport. Add in the impact of cheap overseas holidays in the 1960s, and the overall numbers also began to fall, despite what Tim Newcombe described as the reasonable fares when returning from London.

"I was on a pretty minimum wage, but I always felt that the fare was affordable, which I don't feel now."

Tim also had a system to ensure that he didn't get hungry on the way home.

"I found that if you sat in the dining car at the end furthest from the kitchen, they always offered you everything that was left at the end of the session. It was very generous and very welcome."

The first of the 'holiday' lines to close, in 1960, was that from Louth to Mablethorpe, along with all the stations between the two towns, which it was claimed was losing £10,000 a year. Mablethorpe itself survived because it still had large numbers of visitors, but most of them arrived along the link from Sutton. Some of the track north of the town was retained for storage of coaches during busy excursion periods. The altered service didn't suit Maureen Monk, whose daily travel from Mablethorpe to work in Louth required a change at Willoughby, and a shorter working day.

"I never really put in a full day's work. The train didn't get to Louth until after nine, and I had to leave early to get one home again. On Saturday evening I was often the only person on the train."

The shift to cars and buses, and even more so, lorries for local haulage, caused many closures along the ELR and its branches. Seventeen stations were closed to passengers in 1963, with 22 goods yards going a year later, but a much bigger loss was demanded by Dr Beeching, whose report, in 1963, recommended the closure of the whole East Lincolnshire Line and all its connecting branches as well as most of the southern section of the GN's Lincolnshire Loop. The suggestion was strongly opposed locally, with several groups organising to oppose the plans, but Louth's final station master, Geoff Hannant, felt that closure was inevitable.

"It was an expensive line to run because of all the crossings – that is what killed it. I did the budget for the operations side, which amounted to over £10,000 for a four week period. On top of this was the cost of maintenance of the track, buildings, rolling stock and signalling and telecommunications. It takes a lot of passengers to recoup that sort of money."

"Then there was the freight traffic which, if it were to be profitable, had to be loaded both ways. That is why the fish trains stopped. You could only use the vans one way – they had to return empty because they stank like hell!"

Two public enquiries were held into the Beeching proposals for Lincolnshire. The first, at Skegness in September 1964, considered the original plans, which would have included the closure of the line from Boston to Skegness as well as the other routes in the area. Over 1,700 written submissions were received, many of which included petitions or combined objections from many individuals or organisations. Most were concerned about loss of convenience in their travel arrangements, but

Firsby crossing and station box on 25 May 1970. The remains of the Spilsby line in its final form, cut short with just enough room for a diesel railcar unit, can be seen on the left of picture behind the signal post. *G. Brown Collection.*

some predicted dire economic consequences. One local paper foresaw 'severe heart-breaking consequences to thousands and thousands of people', 'an entire region isolated' and 'economic disaster for the coast'.

A report was submitted to the Minister of Transport, who asked British Rail to reconsider its plans. It did so, and came back with very similar proposals, except that a service would be maintained between Boston and Skegness, partly because of the poor road access to the town. This doubtless sounded more than a little ironic to the residents and prospective holiday-makers at Mablethorpe and Sutton on Sea, which would still lose their trains despite their road access being by narrow winding lanes across the Lincolnshire Marsh.

These 'new' suggestions were looked at by a second public inquiry, again held in Skegness, in May 1968. British Rail claimed that closing the lines would result in a saving of nearly a quarter of a million pounds a year. They argued that the comprehensive network of bus routes would solve most of the local travel problems, and

Brush Type 2 D5574 enters Burgh le Marsh station with a parcels train in 1964. *P. C. Loftis.*

that long-distance coaches would cater for the seasonal traffic to the seaside more economically than a year-round rail service. The passengers, fish and other commodities which went from Grimsby to London would now be carried by an improved frequency of trains by way of Lincoln and Newark with no loss of time or increased fares. The tracks between Grimsby and Louth were to be retained to allow grain to be moved to a large maltings in the town, and a similar short stretch served a sugar beet factory in Spalding from the main station there. A major consideration turned out to be the very large number of level crossing on the lines, all of which had to be manned, resulting in a large proportion of the labour costs of the lines.

Mablethorpe Junction signal box and Stewton Lane level crossing looking towards Louth. *R. B. Wilkinson/A. Ludlam Collection.*

Despite the 1,600 objections, and the backing of local MPs, the Minister accepted British Rail's plans, and closure was set for May 1970, later delayed to October to allow more bus services to be organised. The announcement was made on 19 December 1969, and was described in the local press as 'one of the most ill-conceived Christmas shocks imaginable'

A desolate view of the once-proud station at Louth on 4 May 1975, when the track to Firsby had been lifted.
D. Mundy/A. Ludlam Collection.

Since the last trains ran late at night on a wintry October Sunday evening there was little special attention at the trackside and on the stations. Passenger numbers were low and, with two exceptions there was little ceremony. The first was on the Mablethorpe branch, where a mock funeral party joined the train with a coffin, which was burned at the end of the trip, and the second a special excursion from Grimsby to London and back organised by the Lincolnshire Standard newspaper. Due to a delay on the return journey the special inadvertently managed to be the final train to cover the whole route. It did get a greater level of support, with buglers sounding the Last Post at Alford, fog detonators exploding under its wheels at stations along the route and a crowd of over a thousand people lining the platforms at Louth. The Mayor of Louth commented that 'If the line had to close, this was the best way to do it. It has been a wonderful day, and we thank the Standard for it'. Geoff Hannant saw it differently.

"There were over a thousand people waiting at the station to greet it. If only a fraction of them had travelled regularly on the trains the line might still be open."

Porter Bernard Wolsey, saw the closures as ending a chapter in local history.

"Working on the railway was a way of life and Mablethorpe was never quite the same again after the railway closed. My grandparents worked for the railway, my grandfather was a porter and my grandmother the crossing keeper at Golf Road. They lived in the crossing keeper's house, where I live today."

Track being taken up in the Great Northern Yard, Grimsby on 25 April 1979. Pasture Street runs across the middle of the photograph and the telephone exchange dominates the skyline. This site is now a retail park. *M. Roughley/A. Ludlam Collection.*

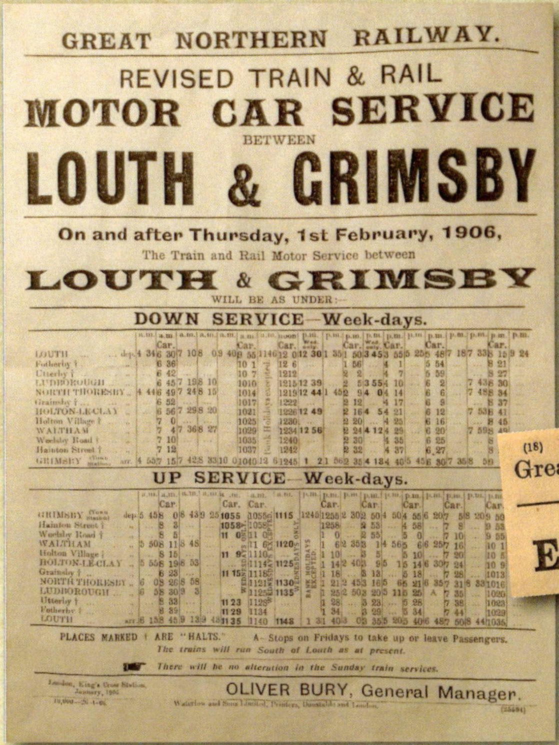

GREAT NORTHERN RAILWAY.

REVISED TRAIN & RAIL

MOTOR CAR SERVICE

BETWEEN

LOUTH & GRIMSBY

On and after Thursday, 1st February, 1906,

The Train and Rail Motor Service between

LOUTH & GRIMSBY

WILL BE AS UNDER:—

DOWN SERVICE—Week-days.

	a.m.	a.m. Car.	a.m.	a.m.	a.m.	a.m. Car.	a.m. (Bank Holidays excepted)	noon Car.	p.m. Wed. only	p.m.	p.m. Car.	p.m. Wed. only	p.m. Car.	p.m.	p.m. Car.	p.m.	p.m.	p.m. Car.	p.m.
LOUTH ... dep.	4 34	6 30	7 10	8 0	9 40	9 55	1146	12 0	12 30	1 35	1 50	3 45	3 55	5 25	5 48	7 18	7 33	8 15	9 24
Fotherby † ...	...	6 36	...	...	...	10 1		12 6	...	...	1 56	...	4 1	...	5 54	...	...	8 21	...
Utterby † ...	...	6 42	...	...	...	10 7		1212	...	...	2 2	...	4 7	...	5 59	...	...	8 27	...
LUDBOROUGH ...	...	6 45	7 19	8 10	...	1010		1215	12 39	...	2 5	3 55	4 10	...	6 2	...	7 43	8 30	...
NORTH THORESBY ...	4 44	6 49	7 24	8 15	...	1014		1219	12 44	1 45	2 9	4 0	4 14	...	6 6	...	7 48	8 34	...
Grainsby † ...	...	6 52	...	...	...	1017		1222	...	...	2 12	...	4 17	...	6 9	...	...	8 37	...
HOLTON-LE-CLAY ...	...	6 56	7 29	8 20	...	1021		1226	12 49	...	2 16	4 5	4 21	...	6 12	...	7 53	8 41	...
Holton Village † ...	...	7 0	...	...	...	1025		1230	...	...	2 20	...	4 25	...	6 16	...	...	8 45	...
WALTHAM ...	...	7 4	7 36	8 27	...	1029		1234	12 56	...	2 24	4 12	4 29	...	6 20	...	7 59	8 49	[illegible]
Weelsby Road † ...	...	7 10	...	...	...	1035		1240	...	...	2 30	...	4 35	...	6 25	...	...	8 [illegible]	[illegible]
Hainton Street † ...	...	7 12	...	...	...	1037		1242	...	...	2 32	...	4 37	...	6 27	...	...	8 [illegible]	[illegible]
GRIMSBY (Town Station) arr.	4 55	7 15	7 42	8 33	10 0	1040	12 6	1245	1 2	1 56	2 35	4 18	4 40	5 45	6 30	7 35	8 [illegible]	[illegible]59	[illegible]

UP SERVICE—Week-days.

	a.m.	a.m. Car.	a.m.	a.m.	a.m. Car. (Wednesdays only)	a.m. Car. (Wednesdays excepted)	a.m. (Wednesdays only)	p.m. (Bank Holidays excepted)	p.m. Car.	p.m.	p.m. Car.	p.m.	p.m. Car.	p.m.	p.m. Car.	p.m.	p.m. Car.
GRIMSBY (Town Station) dep.	5 45	8 0	8 43	9 25	1055	1055	1115	1245	1255	2 30	2 50	4 50	4 55	6 20	7 5	8 20	9 50
Hainton Street † ...	...	8 3	...	...	1058	1058	...	...	1258	...	2 53	...	4 58	...	7 8	...	9 53
Weelsby Road † ...	...	8 5	...	...	11 0	11 0	...	...	1 0	...	2 55	...	5 0	...	7 10	...	9 55
WALTHAM ...	5 50	8 11	8 48	...	...	11 6	1120	...	1 6	2 35	3 1	4 56	5 6	6 25	7 16	...	10 1
Holton Village † ...	...	8 15	...	...	11 9	1110	...	...	1 10	...	3 5	...	5 10	...	7 20	...	10 5
HOLTON-LE-CLAY ...	5 55	8 19	8 53	...	...	1114	1125	...	1 14	2 40	3 9	5 1	5 14	6 30	7 24	...	10 9
Grainsby † ...	...	8 23	...	...	11 15	1118	...	...	1 18	...	3 13	...	5 18	...	7 28	...	1013
NORTH THORESBY ...	6 0	8 26	8 58	...	...	1121	1130	...	1 21	2 45	3 16	5 6	5 21	6 35	7 31	8 33	1016
LUDBOROUGH ...	6 5	8 30	9 3	...	...	1125	1135	...	1 25	2 50	3 20	5 11	5 25	A	7 35	...	1020
Utterby † ...	...	8 33	...	...	11 23	1128	...	...	1 28	...	3 23	...	5 28	...	7 38	...	1023
Fotherby † ...	...	8 39	...	...	11 29	1134	...	...	1 34	...	3 29	...	5 34	...	7 44	...	1029
LOUTH ... arr.	6 15	8 45	9 13	9 43	11 35	1140	1148	1 3	1 40	3 0	3 35	5 20	5 40	6 48	7 50	8 44	1035

PLACES MARKED † ARE "HALTS." A—Stops on Fridays to take up or leave Passengers.

The trains will run South of Louth as at present.

There will be no alteration in the Sunday train services.

London, King's Cross Station, January, 1906.

OLIVER BURY, General Manager.

10,000—26-1-06

Waterlow and Sons Limited, Printers, Dunstable and London. (25594)

Above:
A desolate scene at Burgh-le-Marsh in 1974. *H. Johnston.*

Below:
GNR steam railmotor No. 2 at Louth in 1910 working on the Grimsby-Louth service. *A. Ludlum Collection.*

Above:
Stewton Lane crossing and Mablethorpe Junction signal box in the mid-1960s. *M. Hubbard/D. Enefer Collection.*

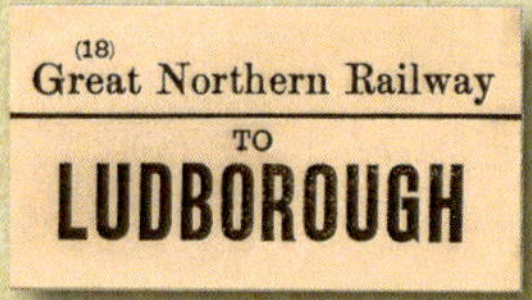

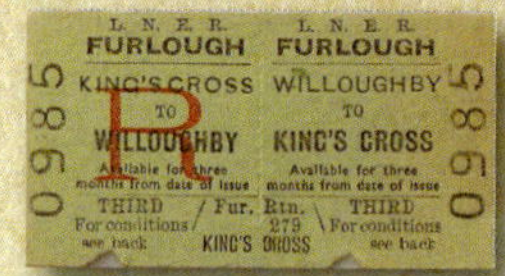

Above:
The impressive frontage at Firsby station pictured in 1970. *H. Johnston*.

Right:
A 1970 scene at Firsby with a DMU on an East Lincolnshire line service passing a classmate on route to Lincoln via the New Line. *H. Johnston*.

Below:
The crossing and classic GNR signal box at Alford looking north in 1970. *H. Johnston*.

The Mablethorpe and Sutton on Sea Branches

Two branch lines opened to the coast from the northern part of the ELR. The Louth and East Coast Railway, from the market town of Louth to what was then a small seaside village, was planned as a farmers railway, to serve the rich grazing lands of the Lincolnshire Marsh. It was not the first proposal for a line to serve Mablethorpe, since Parliamentary approval had been given in 1864 for one that would have linked Alford to what was still a small coastal community. The promoters had become aware of the increasing numbers of visitors arriving by road from the ELR station at Alford, and had hoped to provide a quicker and more comfortable journey, but failed to persuade local investors of their case. The line was not built, but the L&ECR received Parliamentary approval in July 1872, with additional powers granted in May 1877, to serve Mablethorpe and the Marsh by connecting it to the established market town of Louth.

GNR steam railmotor No. 6 at Sutton-on-Sea. *A. Ludlum Collection.*

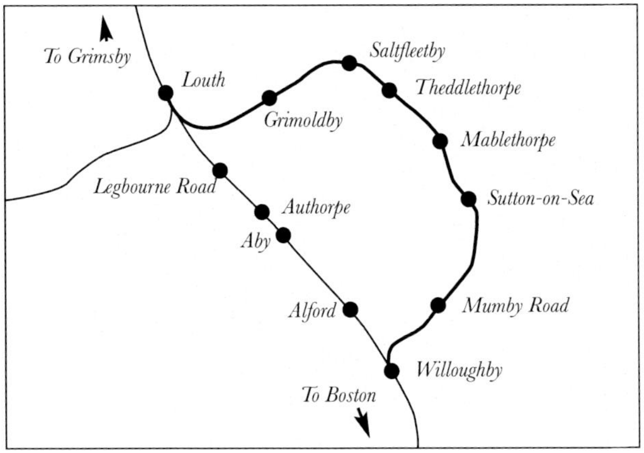

Approval was also given for three small branches off the line, to Skidbrook-cum-Saltfleet, North Somercotes and Saltfleet Haven, but none of them were completed. 13 miles long, the L&ECR opened from Louth to Mablethorpe on 1 October, 1877, and was operated from the beginning by the Great Northern Railway in return for 50% of the receipts for an initial 21 years. Six passenger trains a day ran between the two communities.

The line was single throughout, serving three stations along the way: Grimoldby, Saltfleetby, where double track allowed for a passing place, and Theddlethorpe. It served the local farmers well, with large numbers of cattle arriving by train well into the 1950s, to be fattened on the lush grassland of the Lincolnshire Marsh, and then taken away again for sale or slaughter. To serve that business, cattle wagons were sometimes attached to passenger trains.

The promoters of the earlier line had had the right idea in planning to serve the coastal visitor trade, and an attempt was made in 1873 to restart the project, but Parliament decreed that the L&ECR would be adequate provision. Seaside resorts were becoming fashionable in the mid-19th century, and Mablethorpe and Sutton in the Marsh – rapidly changed to Sutton on Sea – soon caught on to the fashion, despite being described in Ward, Lock & Co.'s guide as 'a flat landscape, a line of forlorn looking sandhills & dull level of shore'! However it did go on to describe 'the cosy nooks in the sandhills, the freedom of the wide sands, the glory of the sunsets over the so called fens, the invigorating air, equalled

An Edwardian view of High Street, Mablethorpe with the level crossing and the station in the distance. *A. Ludlam Collection.*

Saltfleetby station and signal box in the 1950s.
D. Thompson/A. Ludlam Collection.

possibly, but not excelled along these healthy shores of eastern England' which would 'insensibly win the affection of visitors'. 'Pavilions' were erected on the foreshore and other attractions and holiday accommodation soon followed, and the GNR encouraged the company to provide additional facilities at the station to cater for excursion traffic. A link through from the neighbouring Sutton and Willoughby Railway at Sutton on Sea increased the passenger traffic to Mablethorpe, but reduced that coming directly from Louth, although the livestock traffic to Louth and beyond remained very important.

The Sutton and Willoughby ran from the ELR at Willoughby to Sutton by way of a single stop at Mumby Road – a classic case of where adding 'Road' to a station title indicated that it was some distance from the community served. It was originally planned as part of a much larger scheme for a line from Lancashire by way of the East Midlands coalfields to new docks at Sutton, but the docks were never built, and nor was most of the proposed line. The Lancashire, Derbyshire and East Coast Railway did manage to connect Derbyshire with Lincoln later but never served either Lancashire or the East Coast. Incorporated in July, 1884, the Sutton and Willoughby opened 1st November, 1886, although a special train had been run by the contractor, a Mr Dickson, in August of that year, when 250 passengers were carried in wagons to take tea at the seaside – the tea cost 3d (1p) but the fare has not been recorded. Five trains each way served the branch initially, although this increased to seven after the extension through to Mablethorpe opened two years later. The GN was initially reluctant to work the line, which it saw as competition for the branch from Louth to the sea, but eventually did so, taking it over completely in 1902. The L&ECR was also absorbed by the GN six years later.

The S&W was not the first to lay tracks to Sutton. That honour belonged to the Alford and Sutton Tramway, a 2ft 6in narrow gauge line laid in 1884 on the existing roads through the villages of Bilsby, Markby and Hannah. Small tram locomotives hauled what were often mixed trains of passenger and goods stock, with some success. The Tramway therefore opposed the proposed S&W, but campaigners from as far away as Nottingham stressed the case for the more conventional railway. The bill was passed and the arrival of the S&W rendered the Tramway uneconomic, and it closed in December 1889, although a trace of it remained for nearly a century.

The S&W tracks, and the road on which the tramway ran, had crossed on the level, and a trackside hut alongside the level crossing carrying the road bore the title of 'Tramway Crossing', even though the trams had long gone.

The two branches had now become a loop line, with most local trains in later years serving all stations. They survived the financial collapse of the wider national plans and settled down to being holiday branches with year-round local goods and passenger services. In 1889, the year after the connection to Mablethorpe had been made, over 80,000 passengers used the two lines. Passenger numbers fell during WW1, although large numbers of troops were carried to and from training areas near the coast. Direct military action was confined to the passage of a number of German Zeppelin airships, searching for targets such as Grimsby, Scunthorpe and Hull. An opportunity to fight back was missed when an anti-aircraft gun was not used against one of the intruders because the officer in charge of the gun, who had to give the order to fire, had found the local pub more congenial than his action station, and was unavailable when the time came.

Traveller numbers increased again after the war, with about 150,000 passengers carried at their busiest shortly before WWII. The line was one of a number in the area to be patrolled during that war by an armoured train to help defend the coastal beaches against a possible invasion by German forces. The guns were never used in action, although Mablethorpe and Sutton suffered several air raids, including one on Mablethorpe in July 1942, when six people were injured and several houses destroyed or damaged. A rail-mounted naval gun was also based in the area, but its only recorded effect was blast damage to Willoughby station windows while being

Class A5 No. 69803 with a train of antiquated stock at Mablethorpe on 13 September 1954. Note the W. H. Smith bookstall under the station canopy.
P. H. Wells/A. Ludlam Collection.

Table 58 WILLOUGHBY, SUTTON-ON-SEA, MABLETHORPE, and LOUTH

Week Days only

Miles			mrn		mrn	mrn		aft	aft		aft	aft	
–	Willoughby	dep	..	..	8 55	1055	..	..	4 20	..	5 12	7 55	..
3	Mumby Road		..	..	9 1	11 1	..	..	4 26	..	5 18	..	..
7	Sutton-on-Sea	arr	..	..	9 8	11 8	..	..	4 33	..	5 25	8 6	..
		dep	8 25	..	9 9	11 9	..	2 30	4 24	..	5 27	8 7	..
9¾	Mablethorpe	arr	8 30	..	9 14	1114	..	2 35	4 39	..	5 32	8 12	..
		dep	8 32	..	..	1116	..	2 37	..	..	5 34	8 13	..
12¾	Theddlethorpe		8 38	..	..	1122	..	..	..	..	5 40	8 19	..
14¾	Saltfleetby		8 43	..	..	1127	..	..	..	..	5 45	..	..
18½	Grimoldby		8 52	..	..	1136	..	2 53	..	..	5 54	8 31	..
22¾	Louth	arr	9 1	..	..	1145	..	3 2	..	..	6 3	8 40	..

Week Days only

Miles			mrn		mrn		aft	aft		aft	aft	
	Louth	dep	7 44	..	..	..	1 45	3 15	..	..	6 20	..
4¼	Grimoldby		7 53	..	..	..	1 54	3 24	..	..	6 29	..
8	Saltfleetby		8 1	..	..	..	2 2	3 32	..	..	6 37	..
10	Theddlethorpe		8 6	..	..	..	2 7	3 37	..	..	6 42	..
13	Mablethorpe	arr	8 12	..	..	..	2 13	3 43	..	..	6 48	..
		dep	8 14	..	9 20	..	2 15	3 45	..	4 45	7 0	..
15¾	Sutton on-Sea	arr	8 19	..	9 25	..	2 20	3 50	..	4 50	7 5	..
		dep	8 20	..	9 28	..	..	3 52	..	4 51	7 7	..
19¾	Mumby Road		8 28	..	9 36	..	..	4 0	..	..	..	..
22¾	Willoughby	arr	8 34	..	9 42	..	..	4 6	..	5 3	7 19	..

Willoughby to Louth via Mablethorpe Timetable from October 1942.

Crowds queue patiently outside Mablethorpe station for their return train to Nottingham on Saturday 15 August 1964. This photo was used as part of Mablethorpe & Sutton-on-Sea UDC's case against closure of the branch. *F. J. Soar/A. Ludlam Collection.*

fired during practice sessions.

Access to the coast was limited during that war because of the military presence, but traffic built up again afterwards, with 19 excursion trains arriving at Mablethorpe on August Bank Holiday of 1951, and the 50s in general were seen as a second golden age of seaside holidays and excursions.

The lines were also important during the East Coast floods of 1953, when both Mablethorpe and Sutton stations were flooded. Special trains brought great quantities of slag, a waste material from steel-making, from the steel works at Scunthorpe to help restore the defences.

With most excursions arriving by way of Willoughby, and traffic dropping off as cars and buses took away traffic, the line from Louth to Mablethorpe, and the three stations it served, was closed on 3 December 1960. Sadly, a Mrs Lowry, who had travelled on the first train on the line in 1877, was unable to join the final journey at Saltfleetby because of the cold weather.

A view from the footbridge at Mablethorpe of Class B1 No. 61141 with the 12.34 to Nottingham on 9 September 1961.
H. Gamble/A. Ludlam Collection.

A DMU calls at Grimoldby station on 11 July 1959.
H. Priestley/A. Ludlam Collection.

Services continued between Willoughby and Mablethorpe for another decade, but the line was included in the Beeching closures of October 1970. In contrast to the quiet closure of the Louth to Mablethorpe link, when only about 20 passengers rode the last train, the final journey to Willoughby was noisy and chaotic. The platforms at Mablethorpe were crowded with travellers, sight-seers and others, including several amateur hunting horn enthusiasts, who greeted the train and attempted to sound the Last Post as it departed. A variety of wreaths and tributes were laid at the station which carried a notice saying; 'Death Notice. On the 3rd October passed away, at 7:55pm after a long illness, the Mablethorpe-Willoughby British Railways branch line. Passed away – but not peacefully'. Tributes were added to MPs, various councils 'and others who have sympathised in this long illness'.

It is estimated that over 500 passengers travelled on the last train, a DMU with 100 seats, accompanied by a party of mourners with a coffin and a pramful of beer. The train then made an unofficial stop on a level crossing in Sutton to allow the 'funeral party' to get down to continue the wake – and replenish their stock of beer – in a local hotel. It also allowed one Howard Johnston, who had missed the last train, to catch up with it in a taxi, and board it by ladder. He remains an enthusiast to this day.

A DMU waits in the bay platform at Willoughby with the 11.38 to Mablethorpe on 16 May 1970. *G. Gosling/A. Ludlam Collection.*

The last remnants of the footbridge at Mablethorpe are removed after the closure of the line. *E. J. Soar/A. Ludlam Collection.*

Above:
DMU E50036 and 56024 waits at Mablethorpe with a service for Willoughby. *H. Johnston*.

Above:
Mumby Road station in 1970 looking towards Sutton-on-Sea. *H. Johnston*.

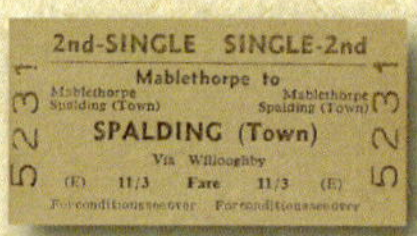

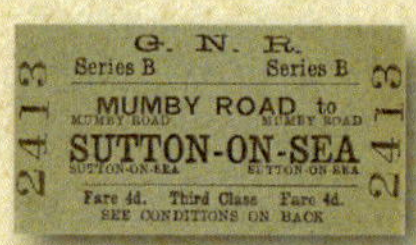

Below:
The same train calls at Sutton-on-Sea on its way to Willoughby. *H. Johnston*.

Above:
The DMU driver prepares to depart from Mablethorpe with a service for Boston in 1970. *A. Ludlam Collection*.

The Spilsby Branch

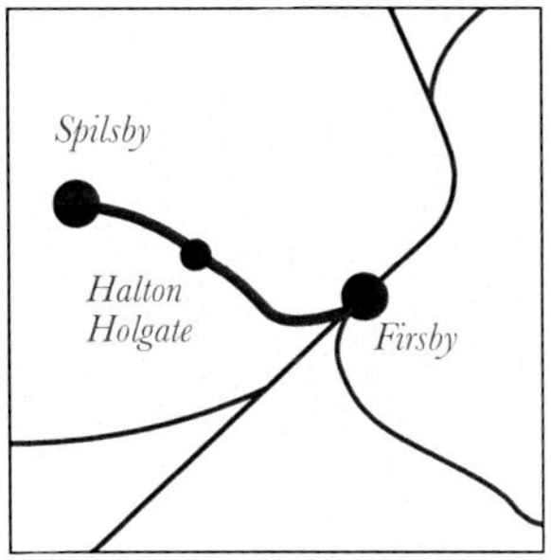

Spilsby, a small market town on the edge of the Wolds, saw the success of the Horncastle branch, and, concerned that market towns with railway services would gain trade from those without, proposed their own line, the Spilsby and Firsby Railway Company. It was authorised in 1865, and opened from Spilsby to a junction with the ELR at Firsby on 1 May 1868, a little later than expected following problems with the contractors, Barnes and Beckitt. The line was just over 4 miles long, and had one intermediate station at Halton Holegate. It was laid to single track throughout, with just one platform face at Spilsby, although locomotive run-round facilities were provided. The Great Northern Railway undertook to operate the line in return for 60% of the gross receipts. Up to ten passenger or mixed trains ran each day with goods and coal or special livestock services as required.

Sadly for the locals, the line was not a success, with no dividends paid on its shares for the first ten years of its existence. Spilsby was only about half the size of Horncastle, and the company didn't have the benefit of an intermediate location like Woodhall Spa, which generated a lot of local traffic. Passenger numbers to Spilsby never reached profitable levels, and the hoped-for boost from the local Partney sheep sales never matched that of Horncastle's Horse Fair, although up to 4,000 sheep at a time had to be marshalled through the cattle dock and into a train of cattle wagons.

Halton Holegate was an even smaller community, although it did generate some business in carrying cattle to and from the rich grazing of the reclaimed marsh-land round the Steeping River. Even that caused some problems, as when a bull being loaded escaped from the cattle dock, swam the river and had what rumour reported was a happy time 'looking after' the cows already grazing there. A number of high quality calves were born later to some of them, despite the farmer concerned not having a bull in the field.

After struggling to attract traffic, the company was sold to the GN in July 1890 for £20,000; about half of

GNR 2-2-2T No. 33 at Spilsby station in 1869. The station shunting horse and yard crane are clearly seen. *A. Ludlam Collection.*

what it had cost to build. The line might have become part of a longer through route if suggestions by Skegness Council, and others, that the tracks should be extended through the Wolds to link up with the Horncastle branch had been taken up. The Council had threatened to link up with the Midland Railway, which connected the Midlands with Lincoln, to provide a new, shorter, route to the sea from Lincoln and the major conurbations further north and west. A Lincoln and Skegness Railway Bill did go to Parliament in 1884, but that would only have put Spilsby on another branch line. The bill was withdrawn later the same year. As an alternative the councils wanted the GN to connect the Spilsby and Horncastle branches, but that company turned them down. Any approaches to the Midland, if they were ever made, never bore fruit. The scheme would have involved expensive tunnelling through the hills, and the link was later made by way of the New Line from Kirkstead to Firsby.

The GN continued to operate the service through the next half century, carrying local passengers, coal, other fuels and agricultural produce, although the frequency of

A panoramic photo of Spilsby station taken from Haw's woodyard. A large Hawthorn 2-2-2 Single No 210 stands in the station. Footplate crew, the guard and station staff are in evidence, so too the omnibus for the White Hart Hotel and a GNR wagon and horse. The private-owner wagons in the foreground add a fine touch. *A. Ludlam Collection.*

Above: The idylic looking Halton Holgate station looking towards Firsby in June 1950. The station retains its canopy, running-in board and gentlemen's toilet sign. A lamp stands alongside the lever-controlled access to the goods yard and shed. *M. Black/A. Ludlam Collection.*

services fell to seven a day in the 1920s. Goods to or from Halton Holegate faced a difficulty in that the good yard sidings were approached through the goods shed which could not be entered by a locomotive because of the risk of fire. Wagons entering the yard were allowed to roll freely down a slight slope, with a railway man using a shunter's pole employed to apply the brakes at the appropriate time. Wagons leaving the yard were attached to a locomotive on the main line by a cable and were pulled quickly towards the good shed. The cable was released from the wagon just before it entered the shed, allowing it to roll through under its own momentum. The brakes were then applied to prevent it running back again until the locomotive could reverse into the yard to collect it. As was so often the case in those days, health and safety of employees was not a primary concern!

Passenger trains ended on 10 September 1939 on the outbreak of WW2, although the official line was that the service had been suspended 'for the duration of hostilities'. Goods continued to be carried, with the usual wartime increase from suppling materials to RAF stations and military bases in the area.

Table 56 — **FIRSBY and SPILSBY—Train Service Suspended**

Bus and Train Connections

		Week Days only											
		From Grimsby Louth mrn	From King's Cross Peter-borough mrn	From King's Cross Peter-borough mrn	From Clee-thorpes Grimsby Louth mrn	From Grantham mrn	From King's Cross Peter-borough aft	From Grantham aft	From King's Cross Peter-borough aft	From Grimsby Louth aft	From Grimsby aft	From King's Cross Peter-borough aft	From King's Cross Peter-borough aft
TRAIN	Boston .... arr	..	7 39	..	..	11 3	..	2 4	2 50	..	..	..	..
	Burgh-le-Marsh "	7 1	..	8 31	..	..	12 57	..	..	2 24	..	7 25	..
	Firsby .... "	..	..	..	10 6	..	..	..	..	..	..	..	7 13
	Louth .... "	..	..	..	..	..	..	..	..	..	5 25	..	..
BUS	Louth .... dep	..	..	..	..	..	..	..		..	6 0	..	..
	Boston .... "	..	8 15	..	..	11 35	..	3 0		..	..	..	..
	Burgh-le-Marsh "	7 36	..	9 1	..	..	1 31	..		2 46	..	7 31	..
	FIRSBY .... "	..	..	..	10 55	..	..	..		..	..	..	7 55
	SPILSBY .... arr	7 53	9 10	9 23	11 16	12 25	1 53	3 50		3 8	7 0	7 53	8 15

Firsby to Spilsby Bus Timetable from October 1942. By this time train services were suspended.

Passenger services were not reinstated in 1947, with one notable exception, but four goods trains a day ran on a regular basis until 1958, with a brief peak of traffic in cement in 1956 when Spilsby aerodrome's runway was being extended to allow larger aircraft to be used, but the service was reduced to a single out and back trip in May 1958. The exception occurred on 19 November when the Royal Train arrived for an overnight stop on the branch. The Duke of Edinburgh was due to visit an anti-aircraft missile site near Grimsby on the 20th, and spent the night between Firsby and Halton Holegate before departing on the train at about 8.30am that morning. The visit was a Last Hurrah for the branch, which was already doomed for closure. BR had claimed that a bridge over the Steeping that had been a long-term concern for the railways companies responsible for it, was unsafe. The figure quoted to repair or replacement of the structure was claimed to be £20,000, a figure deemed unreasonable for a line that was already losing £4,000 a year! Despite a vigorous campaign by the Spilsby Parish Council, albeit without the backing of the Town Council, the line was officially closed, with no significant ceremony, on 31 November 1958. The final train, which ran the previous day, consisted of two empty wagons and a brake van, hauled by a J39 0-6-0 tender locomotive, and the Spilsby and Firsby Railway Company passed into history. Spilsby station was demolished and the yard turned into an industrial estate, although the goods shed survives as a unit within the complex. Halton Holegate station is now a private residence.

For more information on this branch see the companion volume in this series Branch Lines of East Lincolnshire Volume Three: Firsby to Spilsby, by A. J. Ludlam LWRS September 2015.

The east end of the station layout at Spilsby in the 1950s, the engine shed to the left and the goods shed to the right with the station beyond. *A. Ludlam Collection.*

The branch closure prompted the headmaster of Spilsby Grammar School, Mr. Nesbitt to write the following lament:

"Oh friendly little Spilsby train
Will no prayers bring you back again?
A cry goes up, a sound of weeping
From Halton Holgate to Little Steeping,
Wringing his hands our Mr Saggers
On his deserted platform staggers
And engine driver Barwick weeps
As carriageless his engine creeps
We'll never know a Road Car bus
That will shunt back and wait for us.
No morning bus by chance or fate
Habitually ten minutes late,
(While the rate of our gait up Boston Road
Could never by the staff be knowed.)
Worse, if to school a wheel we get
One can't do prep a bicyclette,
The sixth form can't do 4B's Latin
With no plush carriage to be sat in.
When shall we next that smell inhale?
Hear the euphonious whistle wail?
Or feel the rich luxurious motion
Like a tub on a stormy ocean?
When next behold those windows clear
Those views of Yarmouth grown so dear?
Those baggage racks where t'was our joy
To hoist some luckless smaller boy?
Oh tempora! Oh mores! Woe!
Let us unman the Maginot-
Let Hitler have the Spanish Main
But give us back our Spilsby train."

Alfred Albert Mitchell, stationmaster at Halton Holgate until about 1929. He looks very dapper with his bowler hat and walking cane. *A. Ludlam Collection.*

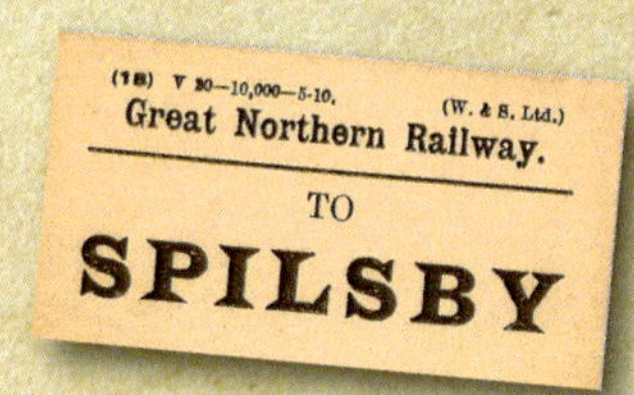

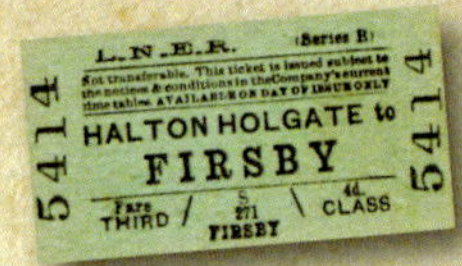

Below: Halton Holgate today, seen from the railway bridge in the photo on page 61. The station building retains its original character, except for the conservatory, which stands on the trackbed.

'Barton's Halt' - formerly the railway gatehouse at Granny Barton's Crossing, between Firsby and Halton Holgate.

The Louth to Bardney Branch

The Louth and Lincoln Railway was another element in the over-ambitious plans for a route from industrial cities in north-west England to new docks to be built on the coast. The failure of that line, and some wildly optimistic predictions of coal and iron resources along the proposed route, saw the company struggle to complete the line or to make any money once it was opened.

Originally incorporated in 1866 to build for 22 miles from Five Mile House on the GN's Lincolnshire Loop to Louth on the ELR, it had to settle for a connection to the Loop at Bardney, less convenient for Lincoln to Louth services, let alone trains to the coast. Seven stations were built along the line, at Kingthorpe, Wragby, East Barkwith, South Willingham, Donington on Bain,

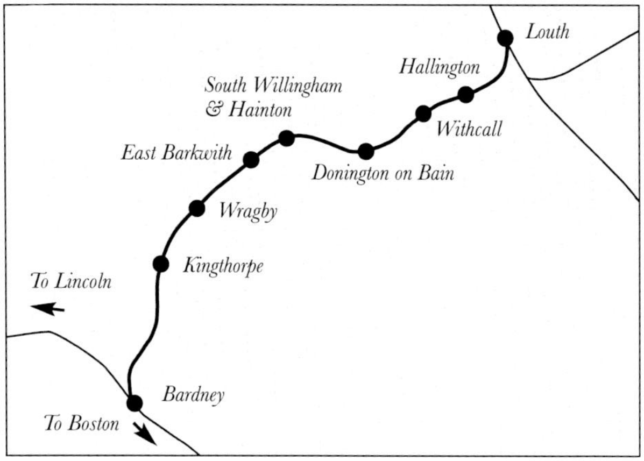

Withcall and Hallington, but the biggest construction problems were the two tunnels through ridges in the Wolds, at Withcall and South Willingham.

A GNR passenger train on the Louth to Bardney branch at some time in the 1870s. *Author's Collection.*

Powers to build the line were received in 1866, but a realisation of the difficulties to be met caused the company to immediately apply for powers to abandon the project. This was refused, and construction began on 1871, but the first section, from Bardney to South Willingham did not open until 1874, with the first through goods train two years later, in June 1876 and passengers in December of that year.

During construction, the company was sold to the contractor that was building it, and then sold back to the company. The GN worked the line from the start, and took the company over in 1882.

It was operated as a quiet country railway for the next 60 years, but then had a brief period of activity as a major supply route to airfields during WW2. A munitions base, known as RAF Market Stainton, was established along a number of minor roads on the Wolds to store bombs and other munitions for RAF Ludford Magna and RAF Kelstern, two stations of Bomber Command. Trains delivered the bombs, with the tunnels on each side of Donington on Bain, the principal supply station, providing occasional cover for loaded wagons.

In the one month of December 1943 more than 1,600 loaded wagons arrived and were sent out to the RAF Stations. This role, and the severe gradients on parts of the line, nearly caused a major disaster in 1944. A train carrying large bombs, which were to be unloaded at various locations along the tracks, stopped at South Willingham, where the guard failed to secure the brakes on part of the train that had been detached from the engine. That section ran away towards East Barkwith, where it demolished the crossing gates and continued

C12 No 67379 stands at the idyllic East Barkwith station on 13 October 1951. *P. Wells/A. Ludlam Collection.*

Donington-on-Bain station seen from the road overbridge in April 1951, seven months prior to closure to passengers. The station buildings are constructed of red brick with courses of buff brick decoration. Donington-on-Bain was on the most beautiful section of the branch between Withcall and Wragby. *M Black/A. Ludlam Collection.*

Table 60 **LOUTH and BARDNEY**

Miles		Week Days only											
		mrn		aft		aft							
	Louth .... dep	7 46	..	1228	..	3 57	..	..	..	..	..	..	..
3	Hallington	Aa	..	1234	..	Aa	..	..	..	..	..	..	..
4¾	Withcall	7 56	..	1239	..	4 8	..	..	..	..	..	..	..
7½	Donington-on-Bain	8 5	..	1248	..	4 17	..	..	..	..	..	..	..
10¼	South Willingham and	8 12	..	1255	..	4 24	..	..	..	..	..	..	..
12¾	East Barkwith ...(Hainton	8 16	..	1259	..	4 28	..	..	..	..	..	..	..
15½	Wragby	8 22	..	1 6	..	4 34	..	..	..	..	..	..	..
17½	Kingthorpe	8 26	..	1 10	..	4 38	..	..	..	..	..	..	..
21¼	Bardney .... arr	8 34	..	1 17	..	4 46	..	..	..	..	..	..	..
30¾	52 LINCOLN .... arr	8 56	..	2 3	..	5 13	..	..	..	..	..	..	..
150½	52 London (King's C.) "	12B30	..	5B55	..	10B2	..	..	..	..	..	..	..

Miles		Week Days only											
		mrn		mrn		aft							
	52 London (King's C.)..dep	4 15	..	7B23	..	1B25	..	..	..	..	..	..	..
	52 LINCOLN .... "	9 17	..	1 5	..	5 47	..	..	..	..	..	..	..
—	Bardney .... dep	9 55	..	1 50	..	6 12	..	..	..	..	..	..	..
4	Kingthorpe	10 2	..	1 57	..	6 19	..	..	..	..	..	..	..
6	Wragby	10 8	..	2 3	..	6 25	..	..	..	..	..	..	..
9	East Barkwith ..(Hainton.	1013	..	2 8	..	6 30	..	..	..	..	..	..	..
10¾	South Willingham and	1018	..	2 13	..	6 35	..	..	..	..	..	..	..
13¾	Donington-on Bain	1025	..	2 21	..	6 42	..	..	..	..	..	..	..
16¾	Withcall	1031	..	2 27	..	6 48	..	..	..	..	..	..	..
18½	Hallington................	Aa	..	2 31	..	Aa	..	..	..	..	..	..	..
21½	Louth .... arr	1041	..	2 37	..	6 58	..	..	..	..	..	..	..

Aa Stops when required. B Via Lincoln.

Louth to Bardney Timetable from October 1942.

In this scene from April 1951, the fireman puts a round of coal into the firebox of class N5 0-6-2T No 69306 at Withcall station before tackling the 1 in 79 climb to the centre of Withcall tunnel. *M. Black/A. Ludlam Collection.*

through Wragby. The signal man there was warned, and opened the gates before the dangerous load passed through at an estimated 40mph. The wagons, and their load, finally came to a rest at Kingthorpe Bottom, a low point in the line, without further incident.

The bomb handling unit was closed in 1948, but not until after another scare in October 1946 when a goods wagon caught fire on a train approaching Donington on Bain Station. Straw packed around a load of gas cylinders was ignited, most likely by a spark from the engine, and threatened to set fire to the whole train. The train crew managed to disconnect the wagon from those behind it and draw it forward, before uncoupling it from the rest of the train ahead. As the freed section moved away, the cylinders began to explode and the burning wagon rolled back onto the coal trucks behind it and set fire to them. The guard and fireman, who had done the uncoupling, were injured by the flames, and both received awards for bravery.

Services did not last long after the war. Formal closure to passengers took place on 5 November 1951, although the last train ran on Saturday 3 November. A wreath was carried on the smokebox door, with the comment 'Born 1876 – Died 1951 In Memoriam'. A large crowd gathered at Wragby to see it depart, and a convivial atmosphere on the train was helped by an impromptu choir from the Gainsborough Model Railway Society singing Auld Lang Syne.

Freight traffic continued for a further five years, and was then gradually whittled back, with the section of the line between Louth and Donington closing on 17 September 1956, and that between Donington and Wragby on 1 December 1958. The last stretch of track, from Wragby to Bardney, was closed to all traffic on 1 February 1960, although a short section, providing access to the canning factory at Bardney, remained open up to the final closure of the Lincolnshire Loop. Little now remains of the line other than the tunnels, some of the station buildings and a wistful thought by many people of what a beautiful route it could have made if it had survived into the preservation era.

Wragby station in June 1951. This was the only station on the line that boasted two platforms and a passing loop. *A. Ludlam Collection.*

Kingthorpe station in June 1951, looking towards Wragby. *M. Black/A. Ludlam Collection.*

For more information on this branch see the companion volume in this series Branch Lines of East Lincolnshire Volume One: Louth to Bardney, by A J Ludlam LWRS 2015.

Above: East Barkwith is little changed from when it was an operational station, the platform edge is clearly seen and the distinctive pine trees in the picture on page 66 are still in evidence to the right.

Above: The 558-yard long South Willingham (High Street) tunnel in 1982. A major landslip occured near the mouth of the eastern end on 21 July 1939.

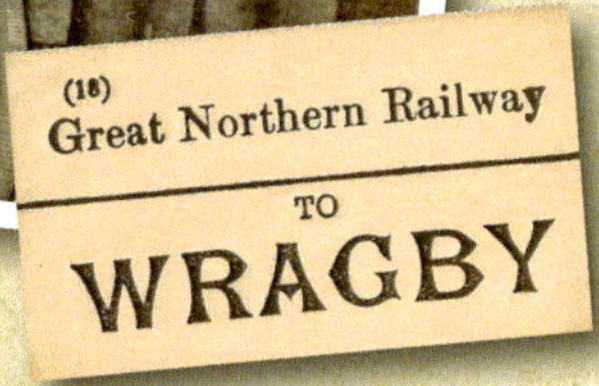

The last passenger train from Louth to Bardney on 3 November 1951.

Donington-on-Bain station today. The shape of the single storey brick building in the picture on page 67, can just be discerned by the slightly lighter brickwork at the near end of the stationmaster's house.

Goods Traffic

Goods were vital to the prosperity of all of Lincolnshire's railways. Passenger transport between major centres tended to be the key selling point for the longer distance through routes, but freight was vital for long and short distance. Village stations became key points for the distribution or despatch of commodities such as coal, bricks, timber, fertiliser and agricultural produce. The price of coal dropped by 25% in Horncastle the year the railway opened, and that town had already got the benefit of a canal, so the reductions in other areas where bulk transport was more difficult would have been correspondingly greater.

Cattle had always been an important business in Louth where animals were fattened on the marshes between it and the sea. The market dated from the reign of Edward VI, and saw dealers buying animals for many distant industrial cities. This trade was hugely facilitated by the branch line to Mablethorpe, which was backed by many local farmers, and by the main line to Grimsby or the south. The railway took a large proportion of this traffic with stock worked in and out of the town, including 30 wagon specials bringing Irish cattle to the area to be fattened on the good Marsh grazing.

Another important local traffic was usually described as parcels or 'less than wagonload' consignments, which were vitally important to local traders serving a wider area and residents needing items only available at greater expense from more distant suppliers. These might be moved by goods or passenger trains, and represented quite an important element in railway finances. Communications to allow for such transactions were also made easier by the use of the electric telegraph, originally used by the railways for train signalling, but later expanded into a major public service, allowing very quick communication of messages wherever there was a rail service.

A Class Q6 0-8-0 passes through Boston with a coal train in the early 1950s. *S. Lathlane/D. Enefer Collection.*

Ironically, that small-scale traffic was one of the reasons that Dr Beeching gave for closing rural lines. He felt that it cluttered up the main network.

"If the proposals in the plan are not implemented we will still get a lot of small consignments of freight – parcels and sundries – that we don't want originating on these branch lines and being handled by these small

Immingham-based class 9F 2-10-0 No 92193 takes the spur to the East Lincolnshire line at Holme Street, with a Saturday London-bound fish train in April 1961. *A. Ludlam Collection.*

stations all cluttering up the network and getting in the way of more profitable traffic."

The most important longer distance freight activity on the lines, however, was the movement of fish, potatoes and sugar beet. The arrival of the railway transformed the fortunes of the Grimsby fishing industry which was despatching 133,791 tons by 1900. A similar transformation happened to the humble potato. Prior to the arrival of the railway they could be a difficult crop to deal with, having to be moved from the fields during the autumn and winter months when the weather could create difficulties. The poor state of the roads and the weight of the crop made it difficult to move it to more distant markets. The GNR was responsible for opening up the market for Lincolnshire growers, offering generous allowances to cover the cost of cartage to the nearest railway station. Given such support the potato industry rapidly expanded. For six months of the year between two and four hundred wagons were despatched daily from Lincolnshire to destinations countrywide and to the ports of Hull, Liverpool, London and Southampton for export. Seed potatoes from Scotland were a major import. The traffic reached its peak between the wars when the six or seven scheduled daily trains increased by two or threefold.

Also at this time sugar beet became an important source of traffic for the railway being moved from most wayside stations to the sugar beet factories at Bardney and Spalding.

A decline in both of these commodities began as

Class B1 4-6-0 No. 61097 at Willoughby with a train of fish empties for Grimsby in March 1963. *M. Black/A. Ludlam Collection.*

Ivatt Class 4MT 2-6-0 No. 43060 with a goods train at Sleaford Junction, Boston in June 1958. *R. C. Riley/A. Ludlam Collection.*

early as 1933 when the railway introduced a system of control which was in conflict with the interests of the producers. The problem was the requirement to know in advance the number of wagons required and the precise times of delivery and collection. This was difficult for the growers who were at the mercy of the weather and could not always predict when they would be able to get on the land to load up. Following an unsatisfactory meeting in the Wainfleet area in 1933 potato growers began to use road transport.

Regular iron-ore trains were worked over the ELR from High Dyke, near Grantham to Scunthorpe steelworks, often using ex-GCR Class 04 2-8-0s.

Class 31 No 31113 has just delivered a vanfit of fibre glass to Associated British Maltsters at Louth on 25 April 1979, and approaches Keddington Road crossing on its return trip to Grimsby. *M. Roughley/A. Ludlam Collection.*

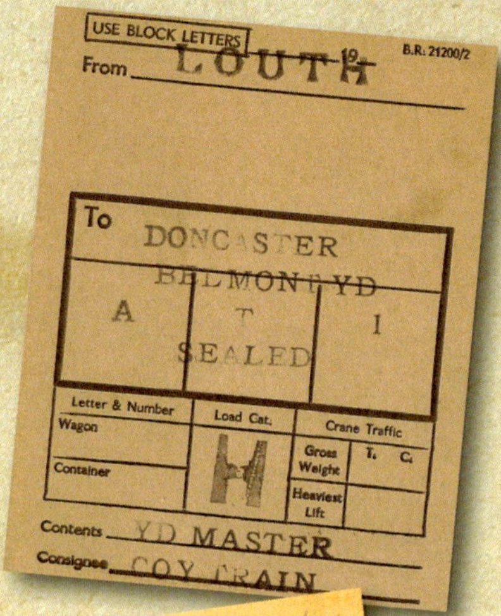
USE BLOCK LETTERS

From LOUTH 19

B.R. 21200/2

To DONCASTER BELMONT YD

A T 1

SEALED

Letter & Number | Load Cat. | Crane Traffic

Wagon

Container

Gross Weight T. C.

Heaviest Lift

Contents YD MASTER

Consignee COY TRAIN

Above:
Class J11 0-6-0 No 64372 heads through Boston towards the Grimsby line with a morning goods in 1959. *L. Perrin.*

O. 6029

POTATOES

LONDON & NORTH EASTERN RAILWAY.

Date

From TUMBY WOODSIDE, L.N.E.

TO DONCASTER

G.N. Section L.N.E. Coy.

VIA

Consignee

Owner and No. of Wagon

No. of Bags

Total Sheets

Whether carriage "Paid" or "To Pay"

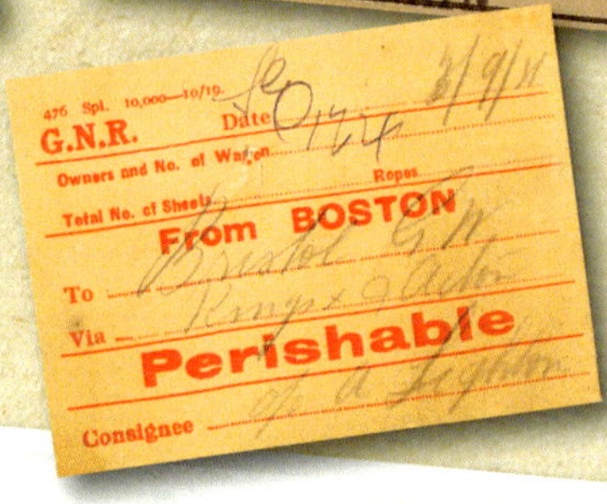
476 Spl. 10,000—10/19.

G.N.R. Date

Owners and No. of Wagon

Ropes

Total No. of Sheets

From BOSTON

To

Via

Perishable

Consignee

Below:
A Great Northern Railway Way Bill for the shipment of goods from Dogdyke to Altrincham.

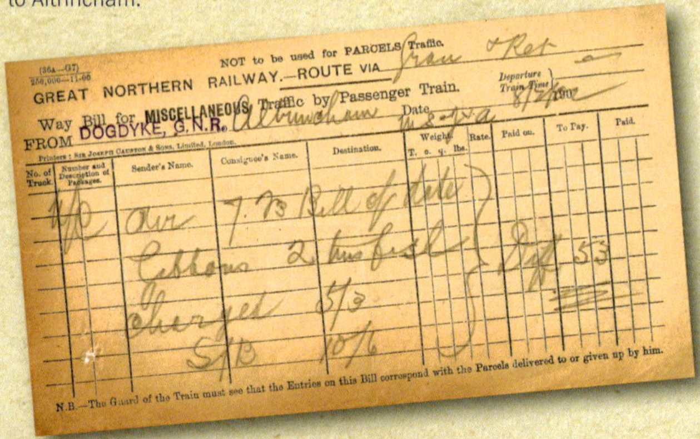
NOT to be used for PARCELS Traffic.

GREAT NORTHERN RAILWAY.—ROUTE VIA

Way Bill for MISCELLANEOUS Traffic by Passenger Train.

FROM DOGDYKE, G.N.R.

Date

Departure Train Time

No. of Truck.	Number and Description of Packages.	Sender's Name.	Consignee's Name.	Destination.	Weight. T. c. q. lbs.	Rate.	Paid on.	To Pay.	Paid.

N.B.—The Guard of the Train must see that the Entries on this Bill correspond with the Parcels delivered to or given up by him.

Above:
Brush Type 2 No. D5835 passes through Firsby station with a northbound freight in 1970. *H. Johnston.*

Motive Power

An interesting range of locomotives could be found on the GNR Lincolnshire lines in their early days. Many of the earliest examples were standard designs offered by established locomotive builders such as Sharp Bros of Manchester, R & W Hawthorne in Newcastle and Bury, Curtis and Kennedy from Liverpool. 'Sharpies' and 'Hawthornes', both in large and small variants, became staples of the company for many years, although most had been rebuilt several times, often as tank engines for branch service, before their final demise later in the 19th Century. Newer classes were also often built by the same companies, but to designs created by the GN's own designers, including Archibald Sturrock and Patrick Stirling.

Working from sheds in Peterborough, Boston, Lincoln and Grimsby, 'singles' – locos with just the one main driving wheel – hauled most of the passenger services, with 0-4-2 and 0-6-0 locomotives with coupled driving wheels pulling the goods trains. The GN did design the '174' class of heavy goods engines specifically for the Lincs Loop, but the length of train they could pull was too great for the stations and sidings on the line, so only six were built.

The most notable of the GNR motive power seen working in the county must surely have been Stirling's beautiful 8ft Singles. They successfully handled trains of 200 tons at speeds of 54 mph and were the GNR standard express passenger locomotive for over twenty years. By 1909 they were becoming a rare sight in London, but were still common in the county as Lincoln,

Stirling 2-2-2 Single No. 4 on a Lincoln-bound passenger train at Tattershall. *Author's Collection.*

Louth and Peterborough engines saw out their lives working over the lines to Boston, Grimsby and Lincoln.

Another class of high-speed main-line engines, Henry Ivatt's 4-4-2 Atlantics worked passenger traffic over the ELR from Grimsby to Peterborough and King's Cross during the 1930s. They could also be seen on the Lincolnshire Loop, although the rather meandering route alongside the Witham did not lend itself to speed, and the demand for it diminished once the Towns Route took the fast trains for the north. 0-6-0 locomotives based at Lincoln and Boston handled goods on that part of the Loop.

As an experiment, the GNR tried running steam rail-motors between Louth and Grimsby, and on the branch to Mablethorpe, but they proved to be unreliable, and were converted into twin articulated carriages, one pair surviving until the end of passenger trains on the

Class N5 0-6-2T No. 69306 waits in the platform at Louth with a train for Bardney in June 1951. *M. Black/A. Ludlam Collection.*

Horncastle branch.

In 1923 the GNR became part of the LNER, and locomotives from other parts of that company began to appear in its territory. A number of what had been Great Central locomotives took up residence at Louth. D7 4-4-0s were there in the 1920s and J11 0-6-0s remained until the shed closed in December 1956, with a Class N5 tank also in residence in the 50s.

The Grouping, as the merger was known, produced an important change in one class of traffic, and the locomotives that hauled it. The substantial Grimsby to London fish traffic was directed over the ELR because it was less congested and more direct than the original GCR route. At the time of the 1923 Grouping heavy fish trains were worked by the powerful Class B7 4-6-0s, but from 1928 the LNER designed J39 0-6-0s were used and later in the 1930s, the Class K3 2-6-0s took over. They in their turn were eventually replaced after nationalisation in 1948 by the new Standard Class 9F 2-10-0s and, around 1961 the Class 7 4-6-2 'Britannias'. The Britannias also worked the morning Grimsby-King's Cross passenger service and its return, taking over from Class B1 4-6-0s.

Before World War 2 Ivatt 4-4-0s dominated passenger traffic in Lincolnshire for many years. Another familiar Ivatt type was the Class C12 4-4-2 tank engines. Initially built to operate the London suburban services, the increasing weights of trains began to prove too much for them. They were transferred to country districts and were associated with Louth and other Lincolnshire locations for over thirty years.

Class J3 and J4 0-6-0s were used on main-line and local goods duties. J3s were still at Boston in 1946. Gresley's Class J6 0-6-0s were familiar in the county, playing many roles: heavy coal trains, local goods and passengers as well as excursions to the coast from the Midlands. Other regular visitors to the area were Class K3 2-6-0s and B1 4-6-0s from Lincoln and further afield, hauling excursions down the northern section of the loop to Woodhall Junction, then taking the New Line to Firsby for Skegness. Yorkshire-based locomotives also regularly turned up with excursions carrying fishermen from there to matches along the Witham and on the large number of substantial drains in the area.

Pick-up local goods trains often had whatever was available for motive power. John Cram remembered using Ivatt and K1 2-6-0s, an ROD O4 63742, a B1, ex-GC Pom-pom 0-6-0s, and A5 4-6-2 tank engines on Boston and Lincoln trains before the end of steam, and

Class 31 and 37 diesels later.

Diesel motive power had reached the county in 1955, although a GWR-built single car had visited on a trial basis a few years earlier. Derby lightweight multiple units arrived in Lincoln in January 1955 and Immingham in July 1956. The Lincoln units were introduced onto the Loop and Immingham ones, based at Cleethorpes, the ELR and branches. They came in gradually, with driver training on the ELR carried out from Grimsby to Boston via the Mablethorpe loop, and return via Alford and Louth. The lightweights were superseded by Derby-built heavyweight units with two horizontal underslung engines and capable of pulling a parcels van or, in some recorded cases, a horse box. Cravens units also operated in various parts of the county.

The faster through trains remained loco hauled for a

B1 No 61201 passing through Woodhall Junction with an excursion heading for the Lincolnshire coast. The picture was taken from the steps of the signal box at some point in the early 50s before the brick goods shed was demolished in 1955. *Marjorie Cook.*

Class 31 No. 31238 at Holton le Clay on 18 March 1976. *P. Loftis.*

while, with fireman Brian Bell welcoming the arrival of the new class of Britannia Pacifics in the final years of steam.

"The B1s were a rough ride, but the Britannias were lovely engines – not quite as good as the older ones on the main line, but a pleasure to work on."

Brush Class 31 diesels were based at Immingham, and were used to replace steam on the Cleethorpes to King's Cross passenger expresses. The original Mirlees engines were very much underpowered for dealing with the heavy fast trains and were eventually upgraded with more powerful English Electric units. Although an improvement they still did not provide the required power for express working. English Electric Class 37s were better locomotives, but the Brush Sulzer 95 mph Class 47s eventually solved the speed and power problem.

The arrival of the diesels ended a traditional ladder of opportunity for locomen. John Cram saw the ending of the need for fireman as 'seriously reducing' the chance of moving through that grade to become a driver, and left the railways. His father, Tommy, already a driver, chose to take early retirement.

Above:
Class K2 2-6-0 No 61759 stands near the coaling tower at its home shed of Boston on 23 June 1958. *R. C. Riley/A. Ludlam Collection.*

Right: Brush Type 4 No. D1763 at Spalding with a Grimsby-King's Cross service on 3 January 1970. *H. Johnston.*

Below: A Class 114 DMU in the northbound platform at Firsby. The station retained its overall roof right to the end. *H. Johnston.*

Above:
Britannia Pacific No. 70040 'Clive of India' at Spalding station in June 1961. *J. Ray.*

Below: Class 47 No. 1577 at Grimsby with the final through southbound train to London via the East Lincolnshire line. *H. Johnston.*